# The Gospel for Loyalists

## A 40-Day Devotional for Dependable, Courageous Guardians

BY TYLER ZACH

*The Gospel for Loyalists: A 40-Day Devotional for Dependable, Courageous Guardians: (Enneagram Type 6)*

© 2021 by Tyler Zach

Edited by Joshua Casey, Stephanie Cross, and Lee Ann Roberts



*Scripture quotations are from the ESV® Bible (The Holy Bible, English Standard Version®), copyright © 2001 by Crossway, a publishing ministry of Good News Publishers. Used by permission. All rights reserved.*

*Scripture quotations marked (NIV) are taken from the Holy Bible, New International Version®, NIV®. Copyright © 1973, 1978, 1984, 2011 by Biblica, Inc.® Used by permission of Zondervan. All rights reserved worldwide. www.zondervan.com The "NIV" and "New International Version" are trademarks registered in the United States Patent and Trademark Office by Biblica, Inc.®*

*Scripture quotations marked (NRSV) are taken from the New Revised Standard Version, copyright © 1989 the Division of Christian Education of the National Council of the Churches of Christ in the United States of America. Used by permission. All rights reserved.*

*Scripture quotations marked (CSB) are taken from the Christian Standard Bible, copyright © 2017 by Holman Bible Publishers. Used by permission. Christian Standard Bible®, and CSB® are federally registered trademarks of Holman Bible Publishers, all rights reserved..*

*Cover design by Fruitful Design (www.fruitful.design)*
*Interior Design and eBook by Kelley Creative (www.kelleycreative.design)*

ISBN: 9798987077344

www.gospelforenneagram.com

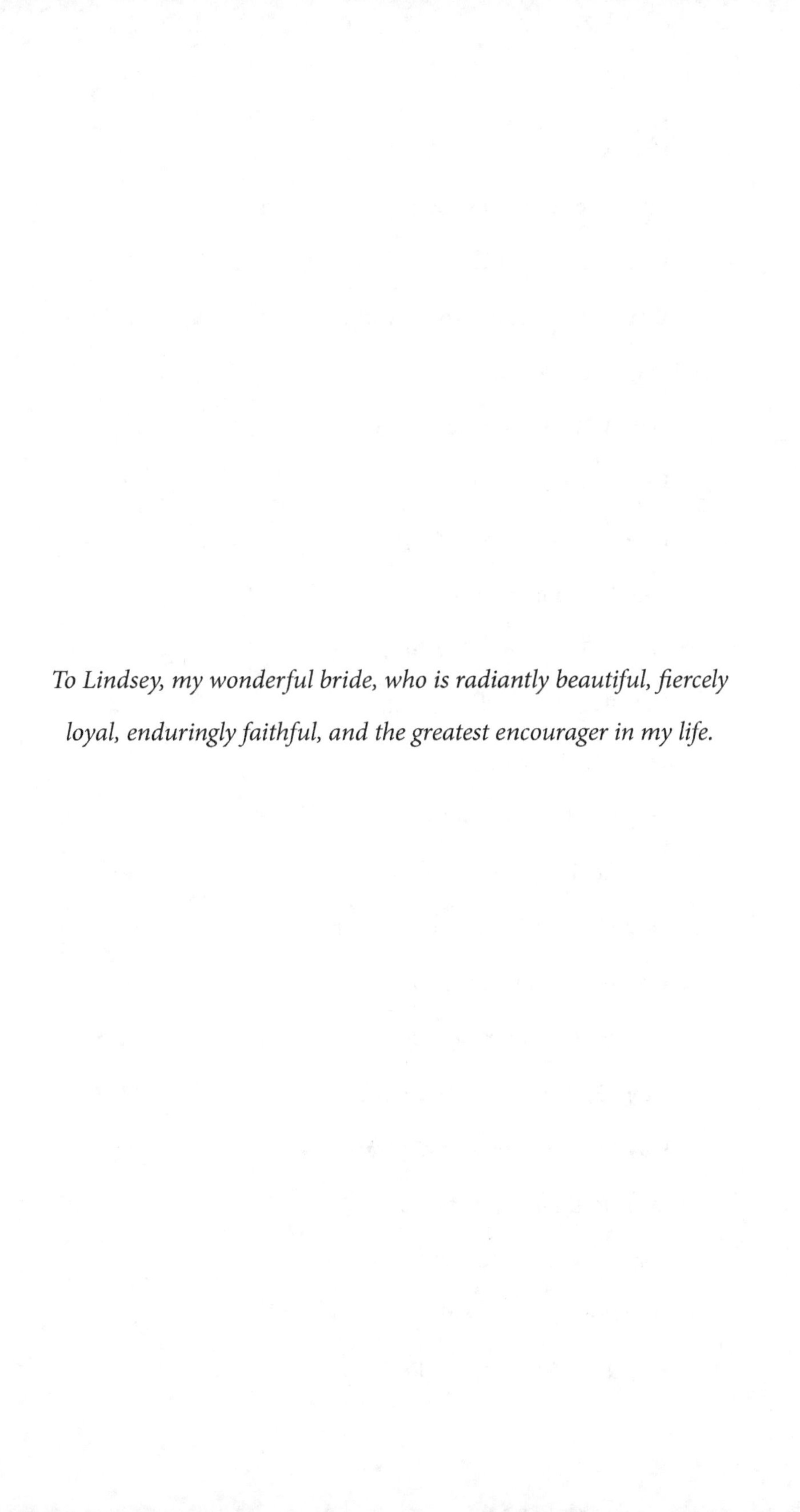

*To Lindsey, my wonderful bride, who is radiantly beautiful, fiercely loyal, enduringly faithful, and the greatest encourager in my life.*

# *Table of Contents*

# *Foreword*

WHEN JEFF AND I FIRST DISCOVERED THE Enneagram, it wasn't easy finding books written from a Christian worldview. We understood how important Gospel-centered Enneagram resources could be, and that inspired us to start our business, Your Enneagram Coach. Since then, we've helped over one million people find their Type through our free assessment, and grow through our online classes, coaching certifications, books, and podcast.

Jeff, my Type 6 husband, brings loyalty, warmth, and playfulness to our marriage. He scans the horizon, so he can safely navigate our family through the ups and downs of life. Despite his struggle with anxiety and doubt, I can always count on him to be courageous when we need him the most. As a Type 9, I also connect to Type 6 through the lines (Enneagram Paths) in the Enneagram symbol. This connection helps me demonstrate courage by stepping out of my Type 9 comfort zone and into unfamiliar areas that help me further my self-development.

The Enneagram is a tool that clarifies our fallen nature while also reminding us we are created in the *Imago Dei* ("image of God"). When Jeff and I understood the why behind our thoughts and actions, it transformed how we looked at ourselves, our relationship with God, our marriage, our parenting, and (obviously) our careers. Taking a risk by starting a business was both exciting and terrifying. We could have easily spun out of control or run out of gas (at times we did!), but knowing the Enneagram, as seen through the lens of the gospel, kept us grounded and on track.

The world needs Type 6s because you are prepared for any situation. You help others see all the possibilities and make the best move forward. You are fiercely devoted to others and care about their security. In times of trouble, you are brave and steady. Your sense of humor and comradery lightens moods and helps others laugh more.

Like all numbers, Type 6s can have seasons of struggle. When you feel stressed, your inner committee makes you doubt yourself and look to outside sources to help you make decisions. The Enneagram can help you quiet your inner committee and recognize the Holy Spirit's guidance within you. Type 6s, we are confident this 40-day devotional will guide you toward a more self-assured and peaceful YOU.

Jeff and I are thankful the Lord has provided more gospel-centered Enneagram teachers like Tyler Zach. Whether you are new to the Enneagram or have studied it for years, we know that you'll find lasting value in this book. On these pages, Tyler's creative wisdom shines, and his focus always remains on Jesus. We're praying that God will meet you on these pages, and you will recognize your inherent value as His beloved child.

Jesus is the author and perfecter of our faith (Hebrews 12:2). He finished the great task He set out to do (John 19:30). A vital part of His ministry was to stay in alignment with His Father, and He did this by setting aside time for rest and reflection. He invites you to do the same, to come away, to separate from the crowds, and BE with Him. Remember, you are loved and valued for simply being you. You do not have to gain Christ's approval. You are accepted right now as you are.

**—Beth and Jeff McCord**
co-founders of Your Enneagram Coach
best-selling authors of *Becoming Us: Using the Enneagram to Create a Thriving Gospel-Centered Marriage*

*Introduction:*

# The Gospel for Loyalists

CAN I BE HONEST WITH YOU? As a Type Three (Achiever) who tries to impress people, I sometimes find it challenging to win over Loyalists. You aren't wooed by impressive words or flashy appearances and you don't extend your trust to just anyone—you might even be thinking to yourself right now, *I'll see about this book.* That being said, I hope you'll allow me to earn your trust. I'll commit to be as sincere and direct with you as I can. There will be a lot of encouragement in this book, but it's not coming from a place of trying to impress; rather, I want to empower you. I was disheartened when I heard one Six share that most of the Enneagram resources out there made her feel like a "fearful deer."

But that's not how I see you. I have a lot of experience with Loyalists because I married a Six! My wife, Lindsey, is one of the most courageous people I know and she has taught me courage, not the other way around. While I have the gift of faith and can run after a challenging vision, she often stands up to challenging people. Though Lindsey is way more warm and caring than me, she is also scrappier. Her mom had to physically hold her back once in a department store from fighting a woman who was "talking trash" about an incident in the parking lot. Often, after a store messes up my order and I'm content to take what I've been given, Lindsey is already on the phone with customer service because no one is going to take advantage of us! I love her dearly.

Sixes are like CIA officers in a spy-action thriller—caring and compassionate toward their family by day, but deadly assassins at night, taking down the bad guys. Yes, this makes you appear more complicated to others, but you make the rest of our lives more fun and interesting.

Over the next forty days, I want to come alongside to reassure you that God has your back in this dangerous world. I want to help you live from Christ's security rather than for your own, which frees you to rest in God's protection and become more vulnerable with others. I want to point to a God who understands all your concerns and helps you learn how to walk through your doubts in a non-judgemental way. I want to laugh with you, persuade you to stand out rather than blend in, and help you channel all that courage to be strong and courageous, running toward the promised land, conquering your giants along the way, and taking hold of all of the successes that await you there.

The Enneagram can be a helpful and necessary part of spiritual growth through self-awareness. Unlike other "personality" profiles, the aim of the Enneagram is to uncover why we do what we do—to help us see what lies behind our strengths and weaknesses. If we use this as a diagnostic tool, allowing the Bible to provide the language for our interpretation, then the Enneagram can produce great change in our lives, relationships, and work.

This is a book about Enneagram types, but don't be mistaken. Fundamentally, I'm a pastor who believes the Bible is the inspired Word of God and is sufficient for all He requires us to believe and do. That said, I also believe God has provided additional insights in fields like medicine and psychology that are helpful in understanding the incredible world God has made. We must tread carefully as we draw insights from fields with limited horizons of evidence like psychology (we still have so much more to learn about the brain!), and as with any anything we come across in this fallible world, we can put on our gospel lens and make use of the wisdom God has poured out on the whole human race.

### What Makes This Book Different?

While there are other projects explaining the Enneagram, the primary aim of this book is to go deeper by applying the truth of God's Word specifically to your type over the next 40 days. If you are suspicious of the Enneagram or know someone who is, download my free resource called *Should Christians Use The Enneagram?* at gospelforenneagram.com. I pray it will help you engage with the Enneagram as a Christian, and then talk about it with others.

Before we get to the daily devotions, let's look at how the gospel both affirms and challenges the unique characteristics of your type.

## The Gospel Affirms Loyalists

God sympathizes with the worldview of a Loyalist. This dangerous world lacks safety and is filled with naive, unreliable, dismissive, and abusive people. We need honest, faithful, and protective guardians who will care for the most vulnerable, be prepared for the worst but hope for the best, teach us how to be team players in a "me" culture, and demonstrate that love is not a fuzzy idea, but helpful and practical. Therefore, a Loyalist will be happy to know the Bible affirms the following beliefs:

- **God created us to be loyal and faithful.** "Let not steadfast love and faithfulness forsake you; bind them around your neck; write them on the tablet of your heart."[1]

- **God created us to be cautious and prepared.** "The prudent sees danger and hides himself, but the simple go on and suffer for it."[2]

- **God created us to be watchful and discerning.** "Be sober-minded; be watchful. Your adversary the devil prowls around like a roaring lion, seeking someone to devour."[3]

- **God created us to be honest and dependable.** "One who is faithful in a very little is also faithful in much, and one who is dishonest in a very little is also dishonest in much."[4]

- **God created us to protect the helpless and defenseless.** "Learn to do good; seek justice, correct oppression; bring justice to the fatherless, plead the widow's cause."[5]

---

1 Proverbs 3:3

2 Proverbs 27:12

3 1 Peter 5:8

4 Luke 16:10

5 Isaiah 1:17

- **God created us to long for safety.** " 'Because the poor are plundered, because the needy groan, I will now arise,' says the LORD; 'I will place him in the safety for which he longs.' "[6]

- **God created us to have eternal security.** "I give them eternal life, and they will never perish, and no one will snatch them out of my hand."[7]

## The Gospel Challenges Loyalists

The gospel also provides specific challenges to Loyalists. Now we'll explore the most common lies Sixes believe and see how the Bible provides much better promises and blessings. We will move deeper into each of these throughout the next forty days.

- **Lie #1: I am not safe.** The worldview of the Loyalist is that the world is a dangerous place and others are out to get them. It's no wonder that many Sixes suffer from pre-traumatic stress syndrome! No matter how bad the world gets, cling to this truth: "The Lord will rescue me from every evil deed and bring me safely into his heavenly kingdom."[8] Do you burn a lot of calories worrying about the state of the world or the lives of your loved ones? God's daily challenge to you is "do not be anxious about anything,"[9] but "[cast] all your anxiety on him, because he cares for you."[10] Living in a dangerous world makes it easy to become suspicious of God's sovereignty. Therefore, repentance for a Six looks like letting go of unfounded suspicions and making a conscious decision to trust "the faithful God who keeps covenant and steadfast love with those who love him and keep his commandments, to a thousand generations."[11]

- **Lie #2: This isn't going to end well.** Because imminent catastrophe could happen at any time, the focus of attention for the Loyalist is on what could go wrong. Sixes are plagued by life's innumerable "what-ifs" and are often led to believe, as the American poet Robert Lowell humorously said, "the light at the end of the tunnel is an oncoming train." But the good news is that whatever life

---

6   Psalm 12:5

7   John 10:28

8   2 Timothy 4:18

9   Philippians 4:6

10   1 Peter 5:7

11   Deuteronomy 7:9

throws at you, "God is our refuge and strength, a very present help in trouble."[12] Because of Christ's presence, God has provided the best possible outcome for your worst-case scenarios. When the core fear of being helpless or defenseless happens, Sixes don't have to be afraid. Paranoia dies in the presence of the Prince of Peace. When Sixes realize they're not alone, the vice of fear gets turned into the virtue of *courage*.

• **Lie #3: I must sleep with one eye open.** Because the core longing of a Loyalist is to be safe and secure, you might believe you have to be "on duty" at all times. Because we serve an all-knowing God, you don't have to wear yourself out thinking about every traumatic situation that could possibly happen. Your job is to prepare for the worst but hope (in God) for the best. Overpreparing won't always keep you from danger because much of life happens outside of our control. As King Solomon pointed out, "unless the LORD watches over the city, the watchman stays awake in vain."[13] In other words, don't place your security in your preparedness but in God's protection. Don't allow worry to become a "safe place" for you, believing more scanning will lead to more security. Instead, say this prayer and go take a nap: "In peace I will both lie down and sleep; for you alone, O LORD, make me dwell in safety."[14]

• **Lie #4: I am loved for being dependable.** Loyalists have a fear of being punished or banished from their "wolf pack" for being deviant. That's why Sixes tell themselves, "I'm good as long as I do what is expected of me." But this is a heavy weight to carry. The good news is that God's love is not dependent on how devoted you are. No matter how well you keep the law, Christ will always keep you: "If we are faithless, he remains faithful—for he cannot deny himself."[15] If you are God's beloved, you can cast out any fear of being punished or abandoned because "fear has to do with punishment,"[16] but Jesus's death on the cross frees you from condemnation for all your past, present, and future sins.[17]

---

12   Psalm 46:1

13   Psalm 127:1

14   Psalm 4:8

15   2 Timothy 2:13

16   1 John 4:18

17   Romans 8:1

- **Lie #5: It's not okay to trust myself.** The childhood message the Loyalist heard growing up was "It's not okay to trust yourself to make decisions or assume authority." It doesn't help that Sixes have an "inner-committee" of voices in their head causing them to doubt themselves and second-guess all their decisions. The good news is you've been given an inner-guidance system called the Holy Spirit who will "instruct and teach you in the way you should go."[18] Furthermore, Jesus has given you "power and authority"[19] to lead courageously, bring healing to the hurting, protest injustice, and tell the wolves in sheep's clothing where to go. Because God did not give you a Spirit of fear but of power,[20] you can "trust your gut" more and see positions of authority as an opportunity to better love and protect the people you care about.

- **Lie #6: My authorities or support structures will keep me safe.** Feeling unable to survive on their own, Loyalists lean on authorities, structures, belief systems, and allies as their key to safety. These perceived safety nets appear to provide insurance and assurance but must be let go of to follow Jesus for "It is better to take refuge in the LORD than to trust in man."[21] The leaders you follow and detailed plans you make are not fail-safe, but Jesus, your Faithful Friend and Good Authority—who remained committed to the Father's plan even unto death—is someone you can trust with your whole life. True loyalty means breaking free from the codependency or blind obedience to your safety nets and remembering that "your life is hidden with Christ in God,"[22] your solid rock and tower of refuge.

As you can see, the gospel will challenge your perception of the protagonists and antagonists in your life. In the Loyalist's kingdom, those who make you feel secure are rewarded. Your "heroes" become those who indulge every concern, don't challenge you to take risks, and praise you for being a realist (not a pessimist!). Likewise, your "villains" become those who challenge you to become a best-case scenario thinker, be more flexible, show up with solutions (not just hard questions), and take steps of faith even when there are no guarantees.

---

18    Psalm 32:8

19    Luke 9:1

20    2 Timothy 1:7

21    Psalm 118:8

22    Colossians 3:3

God's kingdom will not be filled with those who played it safe, but rather men and women who, according to Hebrews 11, are commended for taking giant leaps "by faith" into the things they could not see. In this place, cowardice is exchanged for courage, certainty for trust, fear for faith, and the devil's advocates become God's advocates. In this place, structure submits to the Spirit, success is pursued over survival, and safety is not an end, but the means to a better end: pursuing all of God's bold aspirations for your life. In this place, the anxious let go of their worries and rest "in the shadow of the Almighty."[23]

## The Invitation

When Jesus Christ, the Divine all in all, entered into flawed and limited human history, He started His mission with an invitation: "The time is fulfilled, and the kingdom of God is at hand; repent and believe in the gospel."[24] He explained that to enter the good, eternally renewing life that begins well before the grave, you must do two things: believe the truth and turn from sin. Believing includes acknowledging who God is, who He says we are, and what He has done for us. Turning includes shedding our false worldview, misplaced desires, strong defenses, hide-and-seek strategies, and self-salvation efforts.

If you are ready to begin this incredible 40-day journey and accept God's invitation, then let's go! It will be an enlightening ride of rapid growth in the days to come as you become more self-aware and experience newfound freedom. You will encounter many aha moments as you read profound truths for your type—and maybe even learn something about the people around you. The things you learn about yourself in this book will stick with you for the rest of your life.

## Phobic and Counterphobic

Before we begin, it's helpful to know that Sixes are vastly different from one another (and even themselves from day to day). Though fear is the dominant emotion in all types of Sixes, it is handled very differently from person to person and moment to moment. Phobic (fearful) Sixes will flee from whatever causes them fear while Counterphobic (fearless) Sixes confront their fears to overcome them. Phobic Sixes submit rather than rebel, and Counterphobic Sixes rebel rather than submit. Phobic Sixes minimize their vulnerability by surrounding

---

23   Psalm 91:1

24   Mark 1:15

themselves with a protective individual (or group), whereas Counterphobic Sixes minimize their vulnerability by taking on their opponents (and obstacles) with strength and forcefulness.[25] Paul's disciple, Timothy, is said to have been a Phobic Six and the apostle Peter a Counterphobic Six.

What makes Sixes more complicated for other personality types to understand is that all Sixes may swing on the phobic and counterphobic pendulum depending on day-to-day conditions or life circumstances. They can vacillate between fear and courage, trust and distrust, belief and skepticism, tenderness and toughness, the offensive and defensive. As Riso and Hudson put it, Sixes are an intriguing "bundle of opposites."[26] The following diagram is intended to help you to visualize the phobic and counterphobic swing:

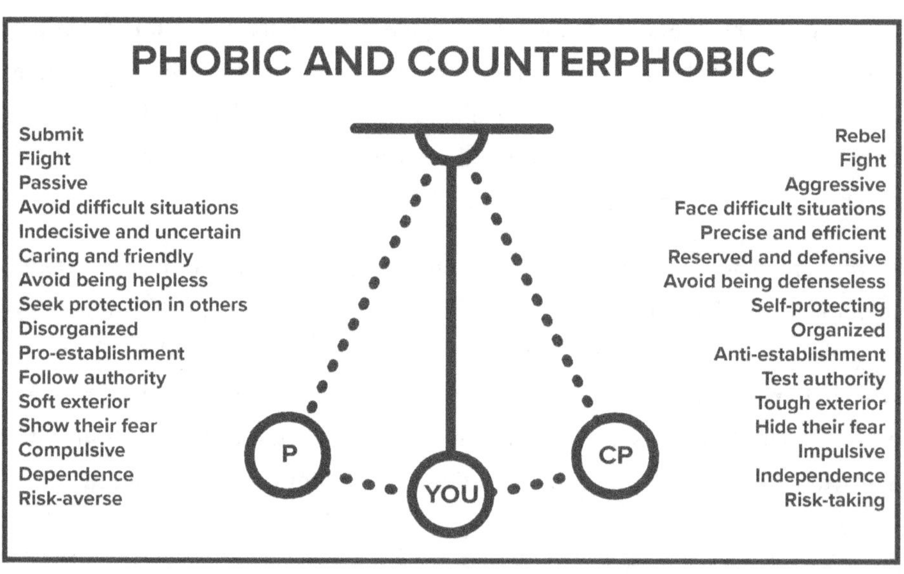



25   Beatrice Chestnut, *The Complete Enneagram: 27 Paths to Greater Self-Knowledge* (Berkeley, CA: She Writes Press, 2013), 195-196.

26   Don Richard Riso and Russ Hudson, *The Wisdom of the Enneagram: The Complete Guide to Psychological and Spiritual Growth for the Nine Personality Types* (New York: Bantam Books, 1999), 235.

## The Three Types of Loyalists

To further explore how Sixes can look very different from one another, please check out the "Three Types of Loyalists" in the back of this book. These "subtypes" are helpful in understanding the nuances of the Loyalist and will explain why some truths in this devotional will hit home more than others. These descriptions tend to err on the negative side, but they are meant to help you further uncover the unconscious motivations driving your behavior and may even help you discover why you're often confused with other Enneagram types!

# Made for Courage

*Be strong and courageous. Do not fear or be in dread of them, for it is the LORD*

*your God who goes with you. He will not leave you or forsake you.*

—Deuteronomy 31:6

---

ON FEBRUARY 24, 1989, CAPTAIN DAVID CRONIN entered the cockpit and began his pre-flight checklist. After thirty-eight years of military and commercial flying, he had only two more flights until retirement. Cronin was assigned to pilot United Airlines Flight 811 from Honolulu to New Zealand. The trip began like any other flight, but roughly fifteen minutes after takeoff—with the aircraft soaring 22,000 feet over the Pacific Ocean—they experienced a major mechanical failure. The giant Boeing 747's right forward cargo door and an adjoining ten square foot section of fuselage tore off, leaving a gaping hole big enough for a semi-truck to drive through. Immediately, nine passengers were sucked out of

> Courage is not simply one of the virtues, but the form of every virtue at its testing point.
>
> –C.S. Lewis[1]

---

1   Gilbert Meilaender, *The Taste for the Other: The Social and Ethical Thought of C.S. Lewis* (Canada: Regent College Publishing, 2003), 217.

the plane because of the depressurization; the remaining passengers and crew reached for their oxygen masks, only to find that the lines had been severed.

With only two of the four engines left and one wing on fire, Cronin got right to work, reducing altitude and guiding the shuddering plane back to Honolulu, saving the remaining 336 traumatized passengers and 18 crew members. Cronin not only saved hundreds of lives, but his experience and example gave rise to many of the airline safety procedures that are still saving lives today. Cronin was celebrated as a courageous hero but said he felt embarrassed by all the attention—after all, he was just doing his duty.[2]

Did you know the same capacity for courage that saved hundreds of lives that day lives within you? It's easy to forget (or even notice) all your small acts of bravery, but trust me—they're there. You are more courageous and capable than you think. It's really unfortunate that Loyalists typically get stereotyped as the personality type most likely to shrink back from a challenge—the fearful dears of the Enneagram. Yet, when I think of Sixes, my wife included, I see courageous heroes.

> You were made to stand up and offer your tender strength to a world in desperate need.

It can be challenging to stand up and say and do what is necessary when all you really want to do is blend in. Sixes are often filling the roles of middle managers: faithful followers who fulfill their duty to maintain order and protect their families and organizations. That's why the symbolic color of Sixes is said to be beige-brown because "It doesn't strike the eye, it doesn't shine on its own, and it fits in with its environment. It's the color of the bark that protects the tree from dangers."[3]

Enneagram teacher Suzanne Stabile shares what a talented Six performer said to her: "We're not special, we're not different, we're just like you. So, when I walk off stage, I don't want people to think I'm awesome or amazing. I want to be able

---

2   Kathleen Maclay, "Crew Describes Saving Flight 811," AP News, March 3, 1989, https://apnews.com/article/866ce15fc1bc3fd0ecb1d195bf48fed3.

3   Richard Rohr and Andreas Ebert, *The Enneagram: A Christian Perspective* (Crossroad Pub, 2001), 140.

to talk to them about their lives and their kids and tell them about mine. I really want them to know I'm just like them."[4]

This desire to blend is truly admirable and often creates the sort of safety and wholeness that allows healthy families and organizations to thrive. However, one pitfall this type must be aware of is the motivation for such blending. Fearful of overexposure, failure, or criticism, Sixes are sometimes hesitant to be thrust into the leadership spotlight because that would mean a bigger target on their backs, or as the old Japanese adage goes, "The blade of grass that grows too high gets chopped off."[5] But God didn't intend for the rest of us to play one long game of "Where's Waldo," trying to pick you out of the crowd. You were made to stand up and offer your tender strength to a world in desperate need. Your purpose is larger than your fear and requires supernatural courage.

***The Good News for Loyalists*** is that Jesus offers a path for such quiet courage. He called into being a community of salt and light—of brothers and sisters who exist to mutually lift one another up and strengthen one another to speak life into a world grown cold. The sort of courage Christ offers is Spirit-filled, giving strength to endure and love to the last; the sort of courage that led Him to Calvary and brought redemption to the world. He calls us to bear His cross as well; to offer hope and humble strength in a posture of open-armed, sacrificial love.

---

### → Pray

Father, help me to see myself as You see me—bold and daring. Give me a resurgence of confidence through the Holy Spirit to rise up and complete the courageous work You've prepared for me. Forgive me for thinking I don't have what it takes to act brave in my worst-case scenarios. Remind me that I can do all things through Christ who strengthens me.

---

4   Suzanne Stabile, *The Path Between Us: An Enneagram Journey to Healthy Relationships* (IVP Books, 2018), 147.

5   Riso and Hudson, *The Wisdom*, 234.

# Day 1 Reflections:

**Describe a time when you overcame your fears and acted brave.**

**How do you try to blend in with the crowd? What drives or motivates you?**

**What leadership role or successful goal are you avoiding because it will put you in a vulnerable spot? How does Jesus free you to engage with courage?**

> **→ Respond**
>
> Search for, listen to, and meditate on the song called "Six" from the Sleeping At Last project.[6]

---

6   Ryan O'Neal, "Sleeping At Last," Sleeping At Last, 2016, http://sleepingatlast.com.

# It's a Dangerous World

*I have said these things to you, that in me you may have peace. In the world you*

*will have tribulation. But take heart; I have overcome the world.*

—John 16:33

THERE WAS A KINDERGARTEN TEACHER EVERYONE LOVED. He had a SpongeBob-themed classroom and all the kids wanted to be in his class. Despite his popularity with students and parents, one student in the school had a bad feeling but couldn't explain why: "This guy made me sick just looking at him," she said. "I would get really anxious around him, and when my friends said, 'Let's go talk to Mr. X,' I would make some excuse to stay away from him." Around ten years later, this teacher made the headlines after being arrested for inappropriate behavior with students. Turns out, this young child did have the right hunch about this elementary teacher after all.[2]

> God's sovereignty had not been shipwrecked by the storm.
>
> —Pricilla Shrier[1]

---

1   Priscilla Shirer, *Awaken: 90 Days with the God Who Speaks* (United States: B&H Publishing Group, 2017), 279-280.

2   Callie Byrnes, "20 People Reveal the Horrible Gut Feeling They Had about Something (or Someone) That Actually Turned out to Be Dead-On," Thought Catalog, March 16, 2018, https://thoughtcatalog.com/callie-byrnes/2018/03/20-people-reveal-the-horrible-gut-feeling-they-had-about-something-or-someone-that-actually-turned-out-to-be-dead-on/.

Have you ever had a hunch or suspicion that turned out to be true? Studies have increasingly confirmed that, even when our minds are consciously telling us everything is okay, our guts often know better.[3] Sixes often have an uncanny discernment about people and situations; they seem to hear their "gut brain" better than most. In fact, I've never met a healthy Six who doesn't have the spiritual gift of discernment. Because of this, it can be a real struggle for Sixes to be around people who won't take their warnings seriously.

Can you relate? Do you ever feel alone because you know the world is a dangerous place but no one else seems to think so? How many times have you shared an authentic concern only to hear the glib response, "Don't worry. Everything is going to be okay"?

> Living in a dangerous world makes it easy to become suspicious of God's sovereignty.

But everything is not always okay. Sometimes, that nagging feeling in the back of your mind (or in your belly) is a warning of real and present danger, whether physical or emotional. One of your gifts to the world is your prudent acknowledgement of these potential pitfalls. As the wisdom of Solomon says, "The prudent sees danger and hides himself, but the simple go on and suffer for it."[4] Even Jesus, who bravely defied ruling authorities, spoke of the need to beware and keep our eyes open, to be "wise as serpents and innocent as doves."[5]

As you scan your environment for danger, it can be tempting to fall into complete despair and feel like you are the lone sheep in a world full of wolves. You may be asking yourself the age-old question, "Why is there so much evil? Where is God? How can He be in control when everything feels so unsafe?" Living in a dangerous world makes it easy to become suspicious of God's sovereignty.

The reality is we all must trust in something; conscious or not, trust is an active, daily decision. Do you trust the Good Shepherd to walk with you through the valley?

---

3   Vanessa Hrvatin, "Our Second Brain: More than a Gut Feeling," Neuroscience, June 10, 2020, https://neuroscience. centreforbrainhealth.ca/our-second-brain-more-gut-feeling.

4   Proverbs 27:12

5   Matthew 10:16

***The Good News for Loyalists*** is that God's sovereignty is stronger than our dangers, and He calls us to a life lived outside our crouching corners. Like Narnia's Aslan, Jesus and the life He calls us to is not safe, but He is good. He warned us to expect trials, not perennially peaceful circumstances. But He did promise we could find our peace in Him. Peace is not the absence of conflict but is an active choice to work even in uncertainty and danger.

Enneagram teachers Ian Cron and Suzanne Stabile say the growth path for Sixes means holding two conflicting ideas in tension: "that they live in a culture that's never going to let them feel safe, and that they are safe."[6] Do you know you are safe in your Good Shepherd's hands? God has your back. I'll say it again: God has your back.

---

### → Pray

Father, I believe and trust in Your peace: help my unbelief. At times, I don't understand why You would allow evil to continue wreaking havoc in this world. It's easy to distrust You when I hear stories on the news or feel unsafe in my own home. Forgive my suspicions and strengthen my trust. Thank You for offering me refuge today under Your protective wings.

---

6    Ian Morgan Cron and Suzanne Stabile, *The Road Back to You* (Ivp Books, 2016), 202.

# Day 2 Reflections:

**When have your first impressions about someone turned out to be true?**

**What potential dangers or dangerous people give you the most anxiety?**

**What would change if you finally let go of the belief that feeling safe is only possible if you can see every threat?**

---

### → Respond

Limit the time you spend watching the news or inputting information from other sources that unnecessarily reinforce your view that the world is a dangerous place.

---

# Loyal Love

*But Ruth replied, "Don't urge me to leave you or to turn back from you. Where you go I will go, and where you stay I will stay. Your people will be my people and your God my God."*

—Ruth 1:16, NIV

IT HAD ALL COME UNDONE. First, A famine swept the land, and Naomi wasn't able to feed her husband Elimelech and their two sons. Out of options, Elimelech decided to move the family from their ancestral land of Judah to the land of their pagan enemies: Moab. There, the boys grew into men and married local Moabite women. Out of disaster, new life was beginning to spring. But tragedy is not done with this family yet. First, Elimilech dies and soon he is followed by both of his sons, leaving Naomi alone in a foreign land with her two Moabite daughters-in-law, Ruth and Orpah.

> God has not called me to be successful. He called me to be faithful.
>
> —Mother Teresa[1]

---

1   James W. Kinn, *Teach, Delight, Persuade: Scriptural Homilies for Years A, B, and C* (United States: Hillenbrand Books, 2009), 17.

Around this time, the famine in Judah ends and Naomi longs to return home to her extended family and native soil. Her daughters-in-law beg to come along, but she instructs them to return to Moab—to find new husbands among their own people, have children, and start again. Even as her heart breaks, she tells them, "it is more bitter for me than for you, because the LORD's hand has turned against me!"[2] Orpah, seeing the sadness but recognizing the sense in Naomi's words, kisses her mother-in-law and turns for home, but Ruth clings to her and replies, "Where you go I will go, and where you stay I will stay. Your people will be my people and your God my God."[3]

Loyalists like Ruth display the *imago Dei* by their fierce faithfulness. The Bible's word for this is *hesed*, often translated as "loving-kindness." Much like God's *hesed*, in the mind of a Six, "Love does." They are unflinchingly loyal and perform many acts of service for their close friends, spouse, children, small group, and anyone else who has earned their trust. Sixes make good on their word and fulfill their promises: if they say they'll meet you somewhere, you better show up because they'll be there. Trust takes time for a Six, but then their motto is, "Once a friend, always a friend."

> When we want to give up on God, God doesn't give up on us.

Sixes will go to great lengths to protect their loved ones and check-in regularly to make sure they are safe and well-provided for and will defend their community or family with more zeal than they defend themselves![4] This simultaneous strength and weakness sees Sixes hunkering down and remaining committed to their beliefs, ideas, or group—even when they are unpopular or when systemic weaknesses are exposed.

Sixes have a friendly, hospitable, often humorous personality. My extremely witty bride, Lindsey, is a Six and I have seen her consistent loving-kindness and care for even childhood friends, always making time for them and remembering to send gifts on their birthdays. Another thing I appreciate about Lindsey is her

---

2   Ruth 1:13 NIV

3   Ruth 1:16 NIV

4   Riso and Hudson, *The Wisdom*, 234.

honesty and genuineness. (I appreciate yours, too!) As a Three who can wear a mask or be performative and pretentious at times, I love your down-to-earth personality that says, "This is simply who I am. Can we be friends?"

***The Good News for Loyalists*** is that although you cannot always depend on others to reciprocate your loyalty, God is enduringly faithful. He knows what it's like to walk with disloyal people, as we see testified in the prophets: "What can I do with you, Judah? Your *[hesed]* is like the morning mist, like the early dew that disappears."[5] But God's loyal love is consistent and dependable.

Ruth, like the God she adopted, displays a *hesed* that is just as counter-cultural today as it was back then. No one would blame Ruth for staying in Moab or moving on and marrying a good-looking, younger man to have a family. Instead, Ruth's *hesed* leads her to follow her now ex-mother-in-law to a foreign land, where she picks up the scraps of grain left in the fields to survive. In the end, Ruth's loyalty changes Naomi. Naomi returns to her homeland expressing a deep, though understandable, resentment and bitterness toward God. By the end of the story, though, she looks back and remembers God's *hesed* and blesses the divine faithfulness. From her story, we learn that when we want to give up on God, God doesn't give up on us—or those whose lives we touch.

---

### → Pray

Father, though my loyalty to You is often like the morning mist, Your steadfast love endures forever. Thank You for creating me to display Your loyal love to the world. I feel Your pleasure when I draw others close and lavish my care and protection on them. Help me see that displaying Your loyalty can turn bitter souls into thankful worshipers.

---

5   Hosea 6:4 NIV

# Day 3 Reflections:

**How are you displaying hesed to your close family and friends?**

**When have you been let down by undependable people? How did it make you feel?**

**Where has the hesed of God shown up in your life lately?**

> **→ Respond**
>
> Research shows that cultivating gratitude leads to increased happiness, better sleep, more energy, and reduced anxiety. Start a gratitude journal to keep track of God's acts of lovingkindness toward you.

# Best-Case Scenarios

*For I am sure that neither death nor life, nor angels nor rulers, nor things*

*present nor things to come, nor powers, nor height nor depth, nor anything*

*else in all creation, will be able to separate us from the love of God in Christ*

*Jesus our Lord.*

—Romans 8:38-39

I'M A "GLASS HALF-FULL" KIND OF GUY: always hoping for the best. It feels really good never worrying about worst-case scenarios … until things sometimes literally fall apart. One afternoon, I found myself on the interstate shoulder in my wife's now-smoking Geo Prizm. Minutes before, the engine had begun making clunking noises, followed by some lurching. When I pulled off the road and the poor car sputtered its last breath, I remembered the oil change I'd been "meaning" to do for weeks.

> I am an old man and have known a great many troubles, but most of them never happened.
>
> –Mark Twain[1]

As a Three, I seem to find myself in situations like this quite often—optimism has a dark side

---

1   Alice Fryling, *Mirror for the Soul: A Christian Guide to the Enneagram* (United States: InterVarsity Press, 2017), 66.

that can lead to catastrophic disappointment and disillusion (not to mention poor financial outcomes, such as a broken car).

One of the many reasons I appreciate the Loyalists in my life is their cautious optimism. To be cautiously optimistic is to be able to clearly see the possible worst-case scenario but allow that to help you achieve the best-case scenario: a safe and secure future. This means healthy Sixes are actually best-case scenario thinkers who ought to be embraced by their families, friends, and communities as their words of caution come from a place of foresight rather than despair. As former Miss Massachusetts Lisa Kleypas jokingly said, "I like pessimists. They're always the ones who bring lifejackets for the boat."[2]

Yet as usual, all it takes to turn a strength into a hindrance is a lack of balance. Unhealthy Sixes fail to see beyond the worst-case, instead seeing "the tunnel at the end of the light" and embracing the proverbial Murphy's Law as a philosophy of life. They may see non-existent threats, overestimate negative data, or catastrophize. Like someone who carries an umbrella in a drought, they may be hopefully waiting for rain or merely adding an unnecessary burden.

> The Bible has provided the best-possible outcome for our worst-case scenarios.

One Six described the exhausting cycle of tension this creates: "When I'm a passenger in a car, I look ahead to see what the other cars ahead of us are doing. I see the possibility of something bad happening, and I imagine a scene of disaster. Heart pounds, pulse races, breath becomes shallow, imagination races out of control—no escape! Nothing happens. I move on to the next possibility. Creating a disaster in my mind is automatic. I can do this for hours, then I observe that I'm doing it and make myself stop, but pretty soon I'm lost in it again."[3]

***The Good News for Loyalists*** is that the Bible has provided the best-possible outcome for our worst-case scenarios. After Jesus—who is clear on His mission— tells the disciples He will have to suffer many things and be killed, the apostle

---

2   Jacqui Pollock, Margaret Loftus, and Tracy Tresidder, *Knowing Me, Knowing Them: Understand Your Parenting Personality by Discovering the Enneagram* (Australia: Monterey Press, 2014), 120.

3   Riso and Hudson, *The Wisdom*, 250.

Peter faces his worst-case scenario—the loss of his friend, Rabbi, and long-awaited Messiah. Unable to see any good outcome, he rebukes the Son of God! Likely, he thought it was Jesus who was catastrophizing; assuming the Rabbi would thank him for the vote of confidence, much like the previous story, when Peter confessed Jesus as the long-awaited Christ. However, Jesus bluntly calls Peter "Satan," telling him to "Get behind me."[4]

As with Peter, so with the world: we struggle with the loss of control and the seemingly endless list of negative results that could arise if we follow Jesus's path of self-sacrificial love. But without the death, there is no resurrection; without the revelation of our inability to save ourselves, there is no trusting hope in the love of God. But because of Christ's path of descent—the true worst-case scenario, being separated from God's love—has been dealt with on the cross and will never be repeated again, and now we all share access to God's "never stopping, never giving up, unbreaking, always and forever love."[5]

> **→ Pray**
>
> Father, though some people think of me as a pessimist I am truly grateful that You've given me Your watchful eyes. Thank You for using my caution to keep those I love out of danger. Forgive me for the times I misuse my gift of discernment and begin problem-seeking. Guard my heart with the peace that comes from knowing nothing can separate me from Your love.

---

4  Mark 8:33

5  Sally Lloyd-Jones, *Loved: The Lord's Prayer* (United States: Zonderkidz, 2018), back cover.

# Day 4 Reflections:

**When has your trademark cautiousness proved to be a life-saver for yourself or someone else?**

---

**When did a situation not work out the way you planned (or feared), but things ultimately turned out alright?**

---

**What is so comforting about problem-solving? How will you prevent yourself from problem-seeking?**

---

> **→ Respond**
>
> To help cultivate the discipline of remaining optimistic, choose a concerning area or relationship in your life and write down all the things that could go right.

*Day 5:*

# Trouble Shooter

*I am reminded of your sincere faith, a faith that dwelt first in your grandmother*

*Lois and your mother Eunice and now, I am sure, dwells in you as well. For this*

*reason I remind you to fan into flame the gift of God, which is in you through*

*the laying on of my hands, for God gave us a spirit not of fear but of power and*

*love and self-control.*

—2 Timothy 1:5-7

IF YOU'VE EVER BEEN CAMPING, YOU'RE PROBABLY accustomed to starting fires (or watching your outdoorsy friend do it). Dried leaves or twigs are laid down as kindling, followed by twigs, then increasingly larger sticks, and finally, logs. Once the fire's ablaze, you can then get to the good part—sitting under the stars and soaking up a good conversation. Yet all too soon, the once-roaring flames begin to die. Rather than start the process all over again, all you need is to

> Go ahead. Make my day.
>
> –Harry Callahan (Clint Eastwood)[1]

---

1   David Sterritt, *The Cinema of Clint Eastwood: Chronicles of America* (United Kingdom: Columbia University Press, 2014), 127.

bend down, add fuel, and blow on the glowing embers and they will once again burst into flame.

In his second letter to young Timothy, the apostle Paul challenges his son in the faith not to let his fire die. Timothy is exhorted to "fan" into flame "the gift of God," which his loved ones and mentor identified. The gift is already there—the fire is aglow. Paul does not bestow this gift on the young man, but opens his eyes to what was there all along. Timothy's flame, unique according to his own giftedness and vocation, has the potential to offer light and warmth to his people.

You might be asking, "What would it look like for me to fan into flame the gift of God?" As a Six, one of your unique gifts to society is troubleshooting. If we all still lived in the Wild West, you'd be the gun slingin' troubleshooter (sorry for the dad joke!). While everyone else entertains themselves in the saloon, you are the one with your back to the wall, hand on your holster, waiting for trouble to push through the swinging doors. Someone needs to protect the rest of us in this dangerous world that's filled with bullies and bandits who have no regard for the law.

> Loyalists face the worst crises with grit and grace.

Loyalists have a revolutionary spirit and, when healthy, face the worst crises with grit and grace. Within every Six is Goliath-defeating courage that calls out the exploitative authorities' injustices and stands as champion and protector of society's underdogs. Holding an "everyman" attitude, they advocate democratic and egalitarian policies that benefit people on every rung of society's ladder.[2] They are cooperative, co-equal partners, who do not dominate in relationships or treat anyone else as inferior.[3]

Sixes are known for being insightful problem-solvers. Using their analytical minds, they do the research, forecast problems, find the loopholes, and are then calm when the crisis comes. These loyal, reliable, and supportive team players and community builders exercise pain-staking precision in their work and "trust

---

2   Beatrice Chestnut, *The 9 Types of Leadership: Mastering the Art of People in the 21st Century Workplace* (Post Hill Press, 2017), 203.

3   Don Riso and Russ Hudson, *Personality Types: Using the Enneagram for Self-Discovery* (HMH Books, 1996), 227.

the process" more than most. When healthy, Sixes exercise wide-eyed positive thinking, bond with others, cultivate trust, and become self-sacrificing for the people and causes they believe in.

***The Good News for Loyalists*** is that Christ's love inflames your capacity to have the courage to protect. Remember, you didn't start the fire, so you can't put it out! That courage within has been ignited by and is continually fueled by the Holy Spirit. Your only job is to keep fanning the flame!

Before there were gunslingers in the Wild West, there were rock-slingin' nomadic shepherds like young King David. We often think of shepherds as harmless guides walking with their sheep beside still waters, but they were fierce protectors, tasked with hyper awareness even during the dull, endless hours of grazing, ready to beat off wild predators. As shepherd-leader, you have permission to wield your God-given, authoritative staff to protect those God entrusts to you.

Pick up your staff today: Jesus has given us an example and all authority on heaven and earth to call out sin, confront false religion, protest injustice, and tell the wolves in sheep's clothing where to go. Because God did not give you a Spirit of fear, but of power, step into your authority today to love others with your protective presence. Your natural gifts are part of a grand plan to push back darkness, mirroring Christ's mission to protect through self-giving love.

---

### → Pray

Father, thank You for giving me faithful people who have prayed for, taught, modeled for, led, and protected me. Help me to walk with authority through this world and be a protective presence, pouring out the fire of Your love on a world that still falls prey to "the devil [who] prowls around like a roaring lion, seeking someone to devour.[4]

---

4   1 Peter 5:8

# Day 5 Reflections:

**Paul asked Timothy to take inventory of the spiritual deposit made by his mother and grandmother. What spiritual truths and gifts have been passed down to you from your family and/or mentors?**

**Which of the strengths above have been affirmed the most throughout your life?**

**What's one thing you can do to ignite and develop your gifts?**

**→ Respond**

Identify your strengths and give examples of how you are already using them.

# The Ark of Safety

*For you have died, and your life is hidden with Christ in God.*

—Colossians 3:3

HAS ANYONE EVER TOLD YOU YOU WERE just a little crazy for being too cautious? Meet Noah. God told him to build a huge ark without any water in sight. People thought he had lost his mind. At that time in history, with the world on a downward spiral, God decided to hit the reset button. He told Noah, "I have determined to make an end of all flesh, for the earth is filled with violence."[1] But, God was also determined to provide Noah, his family, and the animals (don't forget them!) safe passage from this cataclysmic flood.

> Remember, amateurs built the ark, professionals built the Titanic.
>
> –Author Unknown

Thousands of years later, the apostle Peter connects our baptism to this story. Just as Noah (and baby Moses, newly freed Israel, and others) were brought safely through the waters, so too are we granted safe passage from death to life through the resurrection of Jesus Christ.[2] Jesus is our salvation, our refuge

---

1  Genesis 6:13

2  1 Peter 3:18-22

from danger, our ark of safety: "For you have died, and your life is hidden with Christ in God."[3] In Christ, we are hidden from the divine flood of judgement on our lives of scarcity and selfishness and brought into a world of abundance and, most importantly to a Six, safety.

When we drift from this good news, the temptation will be to build our own arks or to hop in someone else's—someone we see as strong and protective. In this world, there are dangerous people who will exploit your fear: presenting worst-case scenarios, these predators will seek to win your vote, your business, or worse, your faith. That's why you need to see past these tactics and find security in your Savior.

> Don't ask the question, "How will God keep me safe?" but rather, "What is God keeping me safe for?"

One Six, who is on the journey, shares, "I feel settled and at peace when I anchor my life in God, knowing that God is there for me and makes my paths straight. It's exciting to consider myself in partnership with God—that we are in this life together and I can face whatever comes my way. When I remember all the ways God has been my strong tower, I can take shelter there. I feel like a baby bird being cared for by its mother. It's very warm and secure under God's wings."[4]

When you feel this settled and at peace, you can begin to think more about your future. Sixes are present-oriented, which enables you to be fully present with others and attuned to their needs. However, when the vice of fear takes over, you could get stuck in the endless negative possibilities of the present—paralyzed by constant expectations of catastrophe.[5]

God is always taking you somewhere for a purpose. Although we have eternal security, right now we have a mission to fulfill. So, don't ask the question, "How will God keep me safe?" but rather, "What is God keeping me safe for?"

---

3   Colossians 3:3

4   Marilyn Vancil, *Self to Lose Self to Find: Using the Enneagram to Uncover Your True, God-gifted Self* (New York: Convergent, 2020), 104.

5   Drew Moser, *The Enneagram of Discernment: The Way of Vocation, Wisdom, and Practice* (Beaver Falls, PA: Falls City Press, 2020), 247.

**The Good News for Loyalists** is that "God is our refuge and strength, a very present help in trouble. Therefore we will not fear though the earth gives way, though the mountains be moved into the heart of the sea, though its waters roar and foam, though the mountains tremble at its swelling."[6] When you are caught in the flood of fearful emotions, picture yourself in the ark. Close your eyes until the storm passes, knowing your life is hidden in Christ. Remind yourself the Lord has "plans to prosper you and not to harm you, plans to give you hope and a future."[7] Fix your eyes on the word *future and* ask yourself, "What would I do next if I had nothing to fear?"

---

### → Pray

Father, with You I feel completely safe. Keep me from pursuing false sources of security in the world that cannot shelter me from my deepest fears. Help me take my eyes off the present and fix them on my future. Just like Noah's ark, I know safety is not my ultimate destination. Take the lead, and I will follow You no matter the cost.

---

6   Psalm 46:1-3

7   Jeremiah 29:11 NIV

# Day 6 Reflections:

**What is security to you? When do you feel you will have enough of it?**

**How might your complicated relationships be transformed if you felt a complete sense of safety with the Lord first?**

**Aside from the dream of having a secure future, what plans do you sense God has for you?**

---

### → Respond

Write out your goals and dreams. Start working toward something that seems impossible without divine intervention.

---

# Promise Keeping

*When the sun had gone down and it was dark, behold, a smoking fire pot and*

*a flaming torch passed between these pieces. On that day the* Lord *made a*

*covenant with Abram.*

—Genesis 15:17-18

WHEN I WAS IN MIDDLE SCHOOL MY father took me to the wildly popular Promise Keepers events. I remember being overcome with emotion as I sang with over fifty thousand men, young and old, in huge stadiums. Promise Keepers is a global movement that calls men to courageous, bold, leadership. However, though the premise of "promise keeping" is a noble idea, it can lead to anxiety when you fall short of expectations.

> Covenants are made for the hard times, not the good times.
>
> –David Gundersen[1]

The Bible calls a binding commitment between two parties a covenant—a promise, pledge, or guarantee that's not intended to restrict, but to protect a relationship. It is an "alliance of

---

1   David 'Gunner' Gundersen, "The Most Important Time to Go to Church," The Gospel Coalition, March 1, 2018, https://www.thegospelcoalition.org/article/most-important-time-to-go-to-church/.

friendship," outlining the blessings and consequences of promises kept and broken. Rather than cultivating fear of punishment, the focus of a covenant is mutual success. I've found that such written, public agreements speak directly to the longings of a Loyalist: Sixes appreciate the expectations that make up these "social contracts" because they offer the security of predictable, good behavior that leads to relational flourishing.

When covenants were made in the ancient Near East, certain rituals were performed to illustrate what would happen if one party failed to follow through on their commitments. Four millennia ago, one such unusual ritual involved dismembering animals, then laying the cut-up pieces in parallel rows. Then, the two parties would walk the path between the animals, essentially saying, "I will be loyal to you, and if I'm not, may I be cut into pieces like this." This sounds dramatic to our modern ears, but they performed this ritual because they took their oaths very seriously—and because there were so few ways of assuring that people of differing social rank would be fair to one another.

> Caring about accountability measures, due process, and clearer guidelines doesn't make you a Pharisee.

With this context, God's actions in Genesis 15 make more sense, mysteriously performing this exact ceremony with Abram. When the sun goes down, God appears as a smoking fire pot and a flaming torch, and passes between the animals. What makes the Genesis story unique is that Abram is not asked to walk the path as well. Oddly, he's not given the opportunity to make an oath and therefore be on-the-hook if he breaks his obligations. Writers like Timothy Keller have pointed out the unique significance of God walking the path alone: God Himself was willing to bear the consequences if Abram was unable to fulfill his end of the covenant.[2]

***The Good News for Loyalists*** is that God is the divine Promise Keeper, who remains loyal to us even when we break our commitments to Him. You may have said to God many times, "I promise I will ..." or "I promise to never again ..." and

---

2    Timothy Keller, "Abraham and the Torch – Timothy Keller [Sermon]," YouTube (YouTube, August 10, 2015), https://www.youtube.com/watch?v=4MLqalGN_ZQ.

are feeling the weight of a heavy conscience today. You may have even felt like a straight-up liar before God because you, like all Loyalists, take your commitments so seriously. But do not fear, God wants you to know that although you will never be able to keep your promises perfectly, He has already prepared a solution.

Just as God stood in for Abram, the Father sent His only Son to stand in for us, making a new covenant. As the apostle Paul proclaimed, "Christ redeemed us from the curse of the law by becoming a curse for us."[3] What this ancient language means for you today is that you no longer have to walk in fear of punishment if you fail to live up to your promises: Jesus perfectfully fulfilled the conditions of the covenant for both parties so you could receive God's unconditional blessing forever.

As you rest in God's finished work, never apologize for being someone who enjoys creating mutually beneficial agreements for your home, workplace, neighborhood, or nation to preserve values and cultivate human flourishing. Without laws, norms, and expectations, we would live in a world with unrestrained evil. Caring about accountability measures, due process, and clearer guidelines doesn't make you a Pharisee, but a reflection of the *imago Dei*.

### → Pray

Father, I praise You for creating the gift of relationship. Thank You for protecting my relationship with You and others with promises of loyalty and commitment. Because I'm made in Your image, show me how I can use my gifts to strengthen the relationships around me. Help me open my heart to receive Your grace today for the times I've failed to fulfill my commitments.

---

3  Galatians 3:13

# Day 7 Reflections:

**What spoken or unspoken promises feel impossible to keep right now?**

**How do you feel, knowing God's unconditional acceptance of you is not based upon fulfilled promises?**

**Have you ever considered that creating "social contracts" (agreements, team norms, policies, etc.) is a reflection of the imago Dei? Why or why not?**

---

### → Respond

Write up a "social contract" for a group of people in your familial, vocational, social, or church sphere to clarify expectations and cultivate trust and mutual success.

# The Lord Keep You

*"You yourselves have seen what I did to the Egyptians, and how I bore you on eagles' wings and brought you to myself. Now therefore, if you will indeed obey my voice and keep my covenant, you shall be my treasured possession among all peoples."*

—Exodus 19:4-5

---

AT ONLY THIRTEEN YEARS OF AGE, MARTIN Luther's parents sent him to sixteenth century boarding school to become a lawyer. However, after almost dying in a lightning storm, Luther had a deeply spiritual experience and changed careers, entering the priesthood instead. As Luther studied his Bible, he became convinced God's grace was not something we could earn by adhering to doctrines and dogmas—contrary to typical Roman Catholic teaching. He sought to reform church teachings, but was eventually excommunicated.[2]

> **God's grace won't abandon you.**
>
> –Christina Fox[1]

---

1   Christina Fox, "God's Grace Won't Abandon You," Revive Our Hearts, May 22, 2018, https://www.reviveourhearts.com/blog/gods-grace-wont-abandon-you/.

2   History.com Editors, "Martin Luther and the 95 Theses," History.com (A&E Television Networks, October 29, 2009), https://www.history.com/topics/reformation/martin-luther-and-the-95-theses.

Because of Luther's battle with Catholic authorities, he remained pessimistic of the law saying, "The law, rightly understood and thoroughly comprehended, does nothing more than remind us of our sin and slay us by it."[3] While I've always loved that punchy quote, I'm starting to realize how much we can use it today to downplay the good aspects of the law. After all, "The law of the LORD is perfect, reviving the soul,"[4] and Loyalists know this truth perhaps better than anyone.

One of the most well-known stories in the Old Testament is God delivering the law at Mount Sinai in an awesome display of fire and storm. God essentially tells Israel (through Moses), "If you keep your end

> No matter how well you keep the law, Christ will always keep you.

of the covenant, I will treat you as my treasured sons and daughters and you will experience blessings only family members are privileged to enjoy."[5] This was a radical concept in the ancient world—the thought that you could know exactly what your god expected of you, never worrying you had to "up the ante" to appease them. What an incredible, peace-giving proposal![6] We learn that "keeping the law" is good because it means each party is doing their part to maintain a stable, healthy relationship.

Furthermore, we see what our relationships should look like before and after the expectations of the law are in place. Watch how God treats the Israelites before versus after Mt. Sinai: as they travel from Egypt, God is abundantly merciful. When they grumble about bitter water, God makes it sweet. When they grumble about food, God gives them manna. When there is no water, God provides water. Shockingly, there are no consequences for their grumbling.[7]

However, once they receive the law on Mount Sinai, their relationship with God changes. God sends fire into the camp the next time they grumble. When the Israelites complain about their heavenly food, God sends a plague. When Miriam

---

3   Martin Luther, Commentary on Romans, trans. John Theodore Mueller (Grand Rapids, MI: Kregel Publications, 1992), XXIII.

4   Psalm 19:7

5   Exodus 19:4-5, author's paraphrase

6   And it literally was—many of the elements in the Sinai covenant's construction became models for the Jewish *ketubah*, or marriage contract.

7   Exodus 15–18

challenges Moses, her brother, publicly, God gives her leprosy.[8] It appears that God held them to a higher level of accountability once they chose to adhere to the law and "knew better."

These stories have significant implications for how we treat people. Christians are sometimes known for being judgmental of those outside the church while overlooking the hypocrisy, abuse, racism, and misogyny found inside the church. It should be the opposite! We need to be radically gracious toward those who have not agreed to enter into this covenant and call Christians who have to a much higher standard.

***The Good News for Loyalists*** is that God's love is not dependent on how devoted to or deviant from the law we are. Loyalists can extend God's grace to themselves and the world Christ died to save, even when both fail to live up to the divine standard. Do you realize God saved the Israelites long before they ever received the law on Mount Sinai? God brought them miraculously through the Red Sea, drowned their enemies, and covered them and carried them along—cloud by day and fire by night—to safety before they had the law! They were saved by grace, not the law. The same is true for us: no matter how well you keep the law, Christ will always keep you.

Even after all the grumbling in the desert, though Israel doesn't keep the law perfectly, God instructs Moses to give them the following blessing. Read it aloud and treasure it in your heart because it's also for you: "The LORD bless you and keep you; the LORD make His face to shine upon you and be gracious to you; the LORD lift up His countenance upon you and give you peace."[9]

---

### → Pray

Father, I worship You as the Law-giver, the One who offered yourself as the reward,[10] establishing covenants with Noah, Abraham, Moses, and David. Help me protect my community by holding believers to a higher standard of loving care and be gracious toward those who don't yet know You or the protective wisdom of Your law.

---

8   Numbers 11–12

9   Numbers 6:24-26

10   Genesis 15:1

# Day 8 Reflections:

**Have you been taught a positive or negative view about the law from your family or church? Explain.**

**What is the significance of the Israelites being saved by grace before they received the law?**

**The apostle Paul exhorts us to judge those inside the church and let God judge those outside.[11] How should this change the way we approach different relationships?**

**→ Respond**

List all the ways you haven't kept the law or fulfilled your obligations. Then rip up the piece of paper and throw it away as a reminder that God accepts you because of Christ, not your obedience.

---

11   1 Corinthians 5:12

# Behavior Modification

*For God has done what the law, weakened by the flesh, could not do. By sending his own Son in the likeness of sinful flesh and for sin, he condemned sin in the flesh, in order that the righteous requirement of the law might be fulfilled in us, who walk not according to the flesh but according to the Spirit.*

—Romans 8:3-4

WHAT DO YOU DO WHEN YOU ARE driving somewhere in a hurry and see a speed limit sign that says, "25 MPH?" Much of the time, Loyalists suppress the urge to break the rules to be good citizens and keep the world safe, ignoring the honks of drivers behind them who would much rather speed through—that is, unless they are feeling rebellious toward certain authorities and become a law unto themselves. The only time my wife Lindsey ever got pulled over was when she was listening to the "Hairspray" soundtrack and took her eyes off the speedometer for a moment—she felt so ashamed!

> You cannot ask the law to do what only grace can accomplish.
>
> –Paul David Tripp[1]

---

1   Paul David Tripp, *Parenting: 14 Gospel Principles That Can Radically Change Your Family* (United States: Crossway, 2016), 45.

Sixes exhibiting phobic behavior will obey to stay safe or prevent themselves from being punished, while Sixes exhibiting counterphobic behavior will push back on laws and rules whose injustices we may be blind to. Generally speaking, compliance with the law isn't valued as highly for other types (with the exception of rule-following Ones, though this is due more to an internal standard rather than adherence to external rules). Not everyone responds as you do when they are exhorted to uphold mutually agreed upon group norms, standards, and procedures. Understanding this dynamic will change everything about how you seek to motivate and change others.

Jesus taught, "For it is from within, out of a person's heart, that evil thoughts come."[2] Jesus makes the case here that all our behavior flows out of the heart. This is critical because, while the law may be able to suppress our behavior, it can't change our hearts. The state patrol can pull me over for breaking the speed limit but they can't turn me into a person who doesn't want to speed!

> When your focus is on Jesus, you'll spend less time fixated on your vice so you can spend more time cultivating virtue.

Timothy Keller asks, "Why do we lie, or fail to love, or break our promises, or live selfishly? Of course, the general answer is 'Because we are weak and sinful,' but the specific answer is that there is something besides Jesus Christ that we feel we must have to be happy. ... The key to change (and even to self-understanding) is therefore to identify the idols of the heart."[3]

Our primary problem is not that we are weak sinners who need to be pushed harder, but that we are strong worshipers who need to be redirected. Knowing this will help you relax your impulse to push what you believe is common sense onto others and become overwhelmed when it doesn't work. While firmly saying things like "stop it" or "obey" is necessary to protect and redirect young children, it becomes insufficient as we get older.

---

2   Mark 7:21 NIV

3   Timothy Keller, *The Prodigal God Discussion Guide: Finding Your Place at the Table* (United States: Zondervan, 2009), 76.

Asking heart-level questions to find out why someone is breaking the rules is necessary to see our own blind spots or help someone break free of their idols. Behavior modification only focuses on surface actions, but looking to the heart helps us seek the Spirit for transformation.

Trying to stop our addictions through behavior modification is like mowing the weeds: they'll just come back again! It's only when we let go of our old desires and replace them with more powerful ones that we'll grow into our new self.

***The Good News for Loyalists*** is that "God has done what the law, weakened by the flesh, could not do."[4] Or as the apostle Paul said: "The law was our guardian until Christ came."[5] Though the law is a helpful tutor in learning God's will, its primary purpose was always to point us to Christ, the only One who can truly change our hearts. This gives new meaning to the old saying, "a good lawyer knows the law and a great lawyer knows the judge."[6] When your focus is on Jesus, you'll spend less time fixated on your vice so you can spend more time cultivating virtue. By beholding Him, rather than focusing on what you or someone else should do, you will be changed from one level of maturity to another.[7] And through the Holy Spirit, you will become someone who honors the spirit of the law without being enslaved to its letter.

---

### → Pray

Father, thank You for giving me the grace and power to change. Help me let go of the belief that pushing people to obey the rules will actually change them. Give me humility to see when the rules need changing and wisdom to understand the ways of the human heart so I can point myself and others to find fulfillment in You. I know You will give us the desires of our hearts if we delight ourselves in You.[8]

---

4   Romans 8:3

5   Galatians 3:24

6   J. Michael Martinez, *The Greatest Criminal Cases: Changing the Course of American Law* (United States: ABC-CLIO, 2014), 56.

7   2 Corinthians 3:18

8   Psalm 37:4

# Day 9 Reflections:

How has behavior modification or "Christian accountability" hurt or helped you on the journey?

What should you change, knowing obedience to the law (or holding someone accountable) is not the end, but a means to a better end?

Are you putting more energy right now into stopping your vices or cultivating virtue? How do you know?

→ **Respond**

Begin practicing one of these spiritual disciplines to proactively cultivate virtue: meditation, prayer, solitude, fasting, study, service, confession, or celebration.

# The Guardian

*Father of the fatherless and protector of widows is God in his holy habitation.*

—Psalm 68:5

ENGLISH WRITER AND THEOLOGIAN G.K. CHESTERSON ONCE shared a fictional story about a town in which the parents built a park for their kids on top of a mountain. On the day of the grand opening, they were bewildered to find the children huddled together in fear rather than frolicking around, having a good time. Some of the parents realized what was happening and built a fence around the park to keep them from falling off the side of the mountain. With this protective enclosure in place, the children started playing heartily and their laughter could be heard all the way down to the town.[1]

> The only thing necessary for the triumph of evil is for good men to do nothing.
>
> –Unknown

This story perfectly illustrates how Sixes help us experience the pleasures of life through the means of loving protection. You nurture and foster healthy growth and development with a parent's heart. You are our guardians

---

1   Jerome Wagner, *Nine Lenses on the World: The Enneagram Perspective* (NineLens Press, 2010), 338-339.

who stand between us and our threats; as my wife Lindsey says, "Your enemies are my enemies."

I think of Loyalists as those who play the role of the immune system in their communities. The immune system is a complex network of cells and proteins that defend the body against external threats. It even keeps a record of every germ it has ever defeated so it can be on guard if those sneaky things come back. This protective system is the basis for immunology: protecting our societies from disease by learning about threats and guarding against them for the sake of those now and those to come. When this system is healthy, it can discern the difference between native and foreign cells; however, if you have an autoimmune disease, your body is deceived into thinking the native cells are the enemy.[2] Similarly, when Sixes are healthy, they are on guard, defending us from attack and fighting for the more vulnerable members. But when unhealthy, Sixes may turn on themselves or others in the body of Christ.

> You are our guardians who stand between us and our threats.

The role of Phoebe, the apostle Paul's trusted partner in ministry, has often been debated in Christian circles. In Romans 16:1, some translations call her a "servant," but the Greek word is *diakonos,* or "deacon"—a specific leadership role in the church.[3] In addition to being identified as a *diakonos,* Phoebe is also named a *prostatis* (Romans 16:2), which is translated here as "a woman set over others, a female guardian, or protectress."[4] In the Greek translation of 1 Chronicles, *prostates* was used to describe King Solomon's officials, and Aristotle used *prostatis* to denote democratic leaders and protectors of the people.[5]

All that to say, Phoebe was more than a wealthy woman who simply bankrolled Paul's ministry! Phoebe may have seen herself as just a helper, but Paul saw her as a leader. Do you see yourself as a leader? Leading does not always mean publicly

---

2   Stephanie Watson, "Autoimmune Diseases: Types, Symptoms, Causes, and More," Healthline, March 26, 2019, https://www.healthline.com/health/autoimmune-disorders.

3   Thomas R. Schreiner, *Romans, Baker Exegetical Commentary On The New Testament* (Grand Rapids: Baker Academic, 1998), 787.

4   Thayer and Smith, "Greek Lexicon entry for Prostatis." "The NAS New Testament Greek Lexicon." . 1999.

5   Darius Jankiewicz, PhD, "Phoebe: Was She an Early Church Leader?," Ministry Magazine, April 2013, https://www.ministrymagazine.org/archive/2013/04/phoebe-was-she-an-early-church-leader

blazing a trail—often it's just the courage to go first, to step out and defend those who follow behind from the dangers ahead. Jesus said, "the harvest is plentiful, but the laborers are few,"[6] but we could also say "the helpless are plentiful, but the defenders are few." The church doesn't need more leaders who love the stage—we need the kind of shepherd who wields their staff well and is so close to the flock that they smell like sheep.

***The Good News for Loyalists*** is we worship *Jehovah Nissi,* which means "The LORD is My Banner."[7] After the Israelites won a close-fought battle, Moses built an altar named "The LORD is My Banner." Remember today that *Jehovah Nissi* is a banner over you, declaring His promise of protection. And when God calls you to protect the people around you like Moses, He will hold up your weary arms until the battle is won.

---

**→ Pray**

Father, thank You for sending Your Son Jesus to get close to the vulnerable, hurt, lost, and even biting sheep. Your banner over me is a symbol of Your love and protection. Forgive me for abdicating my duty when I'm either too fearful to lead or am too skeptical to participate in the body of Christ. Empower me by Your Spirit to live out my role to protect and defend.

---

6   Matthew 9:37

7   Exodus 17:15

# Day 10 Reflections:

**How have you successfully played the role of guardian in your life? Do you see yourself primarily as a helper or leader? Explain.**

<br><br><br><br>

**What makes you angry about spiritual leaders who have no concern for the flock? Have you been more reactive or proactive in dealing with this problem? Why?**

<br><br><br><br>

**Read the story of the battle in Exodus 17. What is so significant about the role that Moses' staff and friends played in the story? How does that give you more confidence to fight your battles?**

<br><br><br><br>

---

### → Respond

Create a list of the most vulnerable people in your family, church, and city. How can you charge the body of Christ to take steps to defend them?

*Day 11:*

# The Myth of Certainty

*Do not be anxious about anything, but in everything by prayer and supplication with thanksgiving let your requests be made known to God.*

—Philippians 4:6

"REMEMBER ... THE FORCE WILL BE WITH you, always." These are the famous words of Jedi Master Obi-Wan Kenobi. Throughout the Star Wars series, Obi-Wan says things like, "I have a bad feeling about this," and "Why do I get the feeling you're going to be the death of me?"[1] Some have likened Obi-Wan's character to a Loyalist because of his famous caution and strict adherence to the Jedi Order.

> We must meet the uncertainties of this world with the certainty of the world to come.
>
> –A.W. Tozer

In his fight against the dark side, we see that Obi-Wan's courage doesn't come from certainty, but rather faith in the force. I'm sure he had his doubts about whether the light would triumph over darkness, but such uncertainties and doubts are not the enemies of faith—they are vital ingredients.

---

1   *Star Wars IV: A New Hope* (Lucas Film Ltd, 2008).

If you pursue certainty to resolve anxieties, you are bound to become more anxious because there is very little we can be certain of in this world. The solution to overcoming the Six's vice of fear is not to chase certainty, but rather to acknowledge your uncertainty—your doubts—and put your faith in God anyway. Having doubts and showing courage, the Six's virtue, are two sides of the same coin called faith. Was Abraham certain he'd be safe when God called him to leave his homeland? Was Gideon certain he'd be safe after God dwindled down his army to almost nothing? Was Mary certain Joseph would treat her well when she revealed her pregnancy? God doesn't seem all that interested in providing us with certainty, but He does ask us to have faith.

In the *Road Back to You*, Ian Cron and Suzanne Stabile point out the important distinction between fear and anxiety: "Fear is what arises when you're in the presence of a clear and immediate source of danger—like when a guy wearing a hockey goalie's mask kicks your door down and chases you around your apartment while wielding a chainsaw over his head. Anxiety, by contrast, is a vague, free-floating sense of apprehension that arises in response to an unknown or potential threat that may never materialize."[2] Do you suffer from constant, low-grade anxieties caused by life's innumerable what-ifs? Does the majority of your anxiety come from the anticipation of future threats rather than real and present danger?

> Paranoia dies in the presence of Peace, not in perceived certainty.

Sixes' responses to anxieties differ widely. Phobic Sixes often exhibit flight behavior, while Counterphobic Sixes will fight[3]—the former responds to fear through avoidance, whereas the latter believes "the best defense is a good offense." Counterphobic Sixes go out and conquer their fears by appearing tough and facing them head on, which is why this type of Six often gets confused with Eights. But unlike fearless Eights, Counterphobic Sixes fight out of deep-seated fear rather than courage (much like the Jedi's dark side enemies).

How can you keep anxiety from driving your life? Think of facts (what you can be certain of) and feelings (what you are anxious and uncertain about) as two

---

2  Cron and Stabile, *The Road Back to You*, 191-192

3  You can find an explanation of phobic and counterphobic in the appendix.

distinct but connected train cars.[4] The engine at the front represents the facts, and the caboose being pulled represents your feelings. Facts are intended to drive the feelings, not the other way around.

***The Good News for Loyalists*** is that you don't have to be anxious about anything because Jesus, who "is the same yesterday, today, and forever,"[5] is with you, always. Paranoia dies in the presence of Peace, not in perceived certainty. Putting your faith in the things of this life leaves a lot of uncertainties, even doubt, but you can have faith in the God who has already saved you, is saving you, and will save you. Don't burn too many calories overanalyzing your real or imaginary woes or foes today. Run to your Father, "casting all your anxieties on him, because he cares for you."[6] Your fears aren't too much for Him.

---

### → Pray

Father, thank You for promising to never leave or forsake me. Help me not to spend my alone time having conversations with all the negative voices in my head. Knowing You care about me, I will bring every anxious thought to You. Replace my desire for certainty with a desire for faith, and let me be courageous enough to thankfully pursue Your love through my doubts.

---

4   Dr. Bill Bright, "Have You Made the Wonderful Discovery of the Spirit-Filled Life?: CRU," Cru.org, accessed October 19, 2021, https://www.cru.org/us/en/train-and-grow/spiritual-growth/the-spirit-filled-life.html.

5   Hebrews 13:8

6   1 Peter 5:7

# Day 11 Reflections:

**What is the difference between fear and anxiety? Where do fear and anxiety habitually show up in your life?**

**Which is worse for you and why: your worst-case scenario actually happening or living with the fear of not knowing what will happen?**

**How can doubt and uncertainty shape your character and relationship with God positively?**

---

### → Respond

Face your fear by describing your worst-case scenario and what would happen to you if you faced it. Next, write out all the ways God might show up to help. Is it as bad as you thought?

# The Inner-Committee

*For God is not a God of confusion but of peace.*

—1 Corinthians 14:33

"DEATH BY COMMITTEE" DESCRIBES THE SLOW AND painful death of an idea or project as a result of disagreements or too much deliberation. Committees of well-intentioned people can be very helpful in accomplishing the mission or they can kill momentum and help bring it to a slow, slogging end.

Loyalists get pulled into committee meetings all day right where they are in their own heads, or in what Enneagram teachers have called the "inner-committee." These unpaid consultants are not loving or patient, but rather relentless with their contradictory thoughts and questions: "That's good, but have you thought about this?" "They might be useful, but don't trust them." Even the most wise and discerning Six will walk out of these inner-committee meetings doubting themselves and second-guessing their decisions.

> Damned if I do, and damned if I don't.
>
> –American evangelist Lorenzo Dow[1]

---

1   Robert Hendrickson, *The Facts on File Encyclopedia of Word and Phrase Origins* (United States: Facts On File, 2008), 227.

Don Riso and Russ Hudson, co-founders of the Enneagram Institute, explain that the key to understanding Sixes is to understand that ambivalence makes them appear like a "bundle of opposites." Generally speaking, a Six may appear strong one minute but vulnerable the next; dependent one day, but desiring independence the next; passive in one conflict, but aggressive in the following one. Though Sixes desire predictability, they sometimes look like the most unpredictable personality type. Will they be witty or cranky, submissive or rebellious, hospitable or interrogating, friendly or provoking?[2] You never know what you will get! That's why I married a Six. I love it when my "sixy" wife Lindsey, who is very warm most of the time, gets sassy and sarcastic on occasion. Life is a lot more fun with her!

While the constant pendulum swinging may be challenging for people who are in relationship with a Six, understanding the source of your ambivalence should give all of us more compassion for you. The generation

> We worship the God of peace, not of confusion.

we live in does not make it easy to live without constant fear or second-guessing; our screens are filled with advertisements invoking our greatest fears and a near-constant sense of lack. Suzanne Stabile illustrates what it feels like living in this world:

> When I watch advertising on television, I might as well give up. I don't have a Bowflex machine. My dishwasher will catch fire any day now. The glass in the shower door is evidently very dangerous. I've been using the wrong toothpaste since I learned to brush. I need to lose weight, but how would I know which system to go with—Nutrisystem, Weight Watchers, Dr. Oz's two-week Rapid Plan, Jenny Craig, or Bistro MD? There is no possible way we've saved enough for retirement. Termites are eating our home from the inside out. And all pork is bad. Or is it chicken? Or beef? And to top it off, the organic vegetables aren't organic. Wow.[3]

Is it any wonder Sixes are so ambivalent? Your natural strength of seeing all options, paired with a culture obsessed with endless options means there are now

---

2   Riso and Hudson, *Personality Types*, 219.

3   Stabile, *The Path Between Us*, 150-151.

exponentially more potential problems—or at least sub-optimal decisions. How is a Six supposed to live in this world?

***The Good News for Loyalists*** is we worship the God of peace, not of confusion.[4] When the Corinthian church allowed too many voices to speak out of turn in their worship gatherings, the apostle Paul spoke up: all of the tongues, prophetic words, and interpretations were creating noise that needed to be toned down, allowing for edifying order in the community. God wants to create the same peaceful atmosphere within your own head: if there are too many voices, know you've been given permission to fire your inner-committee.

Jesus, who clearly named himself as "the way, the truth, and the life,"[5] promised His disciples (and us!) a personal, permanent Guide: "But the Helper, the Holy Spirit … will teach you all things and bring to your remembrance all that I have said to you. Peace I leave with you; my peace I give to you. … Let not your hearts be troubled, neither let them be afraid."[6] When the inner-committee stirs up confusion, lean into your faith in the Guide who leads us on paths of peace.

## ➜ Pray

Father, I praise You for being the God of clarity. Thank You that I can trust and follow You without fear. I am completely helpless without Your daily guidance. Save me from unnecessary ambiguity so I can walk in the peace Christ purchased for me on the cross. Teach me how to listen to the Holy Spirit when there are just too many options and opinions.

---

4   1 Corinthians 14:33

5   John 14:6

6   John 14:26-27

# Day 12 Reflections:

**What does your struggle look like with your "inner-committee?"**

**How often do you consult several people for their opinions? How can you shorten your feedback panel to one or two people?**

**How does Jesus's promise to give the Holy Spirit as a guide bring you comfort?**

---

### → Respond

What are you confused about? Break down the chatter going on in your head into Voice #1, Voice #2, Voice #3, and so on. Then ask for the Holy Spirit's help in drawing a line straight through the voices that don't belong.

# Stop Doubting Yourself

*If any of you lacks wisdom, let him ask God, who gives generously to all without reproach, and it will be given him. But let him ask in faith, with no doubting, for the one who doubts is like a wave of the sea that is driven and tossed by the wind.*

—James 1:5-6

"TRUSTING YOURSELF IS INSANITY" READS THE HEADLINE from a well-known Christian website. The title alone could bring despair to a Loyalist, whose unconscious childhood message was, "It's not okay to trust myself." When Sixes are under stress and paralyzed by self-doubt, their coping strategy becomes relying on someone or something outside themselves for guidance.

> A man who doesn't trust himself can never really trust anyone else.
>
> —Cardinal de Retz[1]

As Marilyn Vancil puts it: "Their gift of loyalty is altered into a dependence on other people or institutions to tell them what to believe, how to behave, and who they should be."[2]

---

1   Riso and Hudson, *The Wisdom*, 232.

2   Vancil, *Self to Lose Self to Find*, 107.

When Sixes are healthy, they engage life confidently like Deborah—the famous Old Testament judge, prophetess, and self-titled "a mother in Israel."[3] As someone who heard countless cases everyday, Deborah had to make quick and fast decisions without much support or guidance. In Judges 4, she summons Barak, the commander of Israel's army, and asks him why he hasn't gone into battle after the Lord commanded him to do so. One can hardly blame Barak: King Jaban had oppressed Israel for twenty years and had nine-hundred chariots that could slice through foot soldiers like butter. Have you ever been in a position like Barak where you clearly knew God wanted you to do something but faced insurmountable fear?

As her people's leader, Deborah takes charge, publicly calling out her countryman and lighting a fire under him to obey the Lord's clear command. We need more Deborahs in the church today to hold leaders accountable! Rather than circumventing his responsibility, Deborah gives Barak the opportunity to fulfill his obligation to protect Israel, but the commander has a condition: "If you will go with me, I will go, but if you will not go with me, I will not go."[4] Barak finds Deborah to be a source of spiritual strength, but his lack of faith comes at a cost: Deborah will receive the credit when the battle is won. With this decided, Deborah advances with Barak and his army and watches the Lord deliver their oppressive enemy into their hands. Later, they even sit down together for a songwriting session.[5]

> Just think about how much easier trusting your decisions would be if you knew you could change your mind later without penalty.

Do you want to be able to trust yourself to make hard decisions day after day without needing feedback on every decision or asking for permission? We'll cover the practicalities of decision-making tomorrow, but for now, meditate on today's story. If you don't want to be tossed to and fro by the winds of ambivalence, you must learn to trust in the face of uncertainty. Rather than fearing that God is out

---

3   Judges 5:7

4   Judges 4:8

5   Judges 5

to catch and punish you in your failure, develop trust that He wants to help you make the right decisions.

Just think about how much easier trusting your decisions would be if you knew you could change your mind later without penalty and receive grace for every wrong choice! Deborah was so decisive because she knew that not deciding is a decision. In short, she felt confident life would be okay if she made a few mistakes and held her ultimate trust in God above her successes and possible failures.

***The Good News for Loyalists*** is you can trust yourself when you are trusting in the Lord. King Solomon said, "Trust in the LORD with all your heart, and do not lean on your own understanding. In all your ways acknowledge Him, and he will make straight your paths."[6] Not leaning on your own understanding does not mean deferring or double-checking all your decisions—that's insanity. The Scripture, instead, means we are to live a life keeping God's heart in focus rather than taking cues from our old attitudes, thoughts, and behaviors.

If you are taking small and steady steps over time to learn God's Word, put yourself next to wise people, and ask the Holy Spirit for help, then you can be fully confident that God is building a library of wisdom within you to draw upon for every circumstance life throws at you. Even if things don't go as expected, take solace in the fact that God will be there to pick you up and keep you on your way.

---

### → Pray

Father, out of Your mouth comes wisdom and understanding. Help me to trust myself more when I'm trusting in You. Forgive me for deferring the authority You've given me to others to make decisions I'm capable of making. Grow my self-confidence so I can use the wisdom You've given me to serve the people around me like Deborah did.

---

6  Proverbs 3:5-6

# Day 13 Reflections:

**Where do you think you got the idea "It's not okay to trust myself?"**

**Why do you doubt that you have what it takes to make the right decisions? What does that reveal about your relationship with God?**

**How would decision-making become easier if you knew you could change your mind later without penalty and receive grace for every bad decision?**

---

**➔ Respond**

Make a decision without asking for help. Try to catch yourself in the act if you ask someone a question to see if it supports the decision you've already made in your head.

# Making Decisions

*I will instruct you and teach you in the way you should go; I will counsel you*

*with my eye upon you.*

—Psalm 32:8

YOU HAVE A DECISION TO MAKE. FEELINGS are churning in your gut, your chest is tight, your palms are sweaty. Lots of competing voices are shouting in your head. You make up your mind, only to change it a short while later. Then, at last, you finally make a decision. You are certain this is the one—then you become skeptical of being too certain: No one can be that certain, I must be wrong. Does that sound a little too familiar?

> Decisions become easier when your will to please God outweighs your will to please the world.
>
> –Anso Coetzer[1]

You are a better decision-maker than you might give yourself credit for. Loyalists provide balance and pragmatism; in fact, every team or staff or committee needs a Six! People who will look before they leap, thinking long and hard about all the possible scenarios. You offer prudence,

---

1 Richie Hughes, *Start Here, Go Anywhere: Making Good Choices, Recovering from Bad Ones* (United States: Charisma Media, 2011), 10.

caution, propriety, and a deep regard for all who might be affected by a big decision.[2] Rather than thinking about fame or fortune, you help whatever team you're on to advance together with the least amount of risk.

But what do you need to be mindful of when making decisions? Generally speaking, Sixes may vacillate between uncertainty and being too certain. Though their natural bent is to take every option under consideration, Sixes may find themselves being overly sure about the "tried and true" methods or values they inherited from their family, church, or tradition. Though Sixes use their heads to take in information, Enneagram teacher Suzanee Stabile explains how they may process that information too narrowly.[3] When safety is the ultimate concern, Sixes may become reductive, feeling it's necessary to put everything (and everyone) in a dualistic, "right or wrong," "good or bad" box to better protect themselves and loved ones.

> You are a better decision-maker than you might give yourself credit for.

One of the villains of decision making is getting stuck in narrow framing—the tendency to define our choices too narrowly because we see the world in binary terms. Stabile recommends reading the words of people you disagree with and listening to news channels that don't condone your views to escape the mentality that there is only one right way. Perhaps that "other" political party or Christian denomination or leader you've been suspicious about may be right about some things. If nothing else, they may help you see your own views in a new light.

A close relative of the narrow framing villain is confirmation bias. This villain will encourage you to do what you always do—go out and consult others to help you make a decision. However, the reality is that if you don't intentionally discipline yourself to consult people who will challenge you, you'll end up speaking only to people who share your bias, confirming the decision you've already made in your mind.[4]

---

2   Wagner, *Nine Lenses*, 339.

3   Suzanne Stabile, Episode 59: The Enneagram and Repressed Centers, podcast audio, June 5, 2019, https://www.theenneagramjourney.org/podcast/2019/episode59.

4   Chip Heath and Dan Heath, *Decisive: How to Make Better Choices in Life and Work* (United States: Crown, 2013).

How can you overcome these villains while avoiding the opposite challenge of analysis paralysis? The most important long-term strategy is to cultivate the character of Christ, humbly depending on the Spirit for guidance. When those two processes are in place, you can then use the following ten guiding questions for support. I've compiled them for you to both affirm what you naturally do and stretch your usual thinking.

1.  What are my realistic options?

2.  When does this need to be decided?

3.  Does Scripture say anything about this directly? If so, what?

4.  What course of action will practically help me love God and others?

5.  What kind of person typically chooses this course of action?

6.  What are my primary motivators in this scenario?

7.  What are the best arguments against this course of action?

8.  What might be the long-term consequences?

9.  What are my trusted authorities saying?

10. What is my conscience telling me to do?

***The Good News for Loyalists*** is that you have been given the "mind of Christ"[5] so that you may think rightly, and the Spirit of Christ so that you may act rightly. Did you know you can make hard decisions with complete peace of mind? Read this promise out loud today: "And the peace of God, which surpasses all understanding, will guard your hearts and your minds in Christ Jesus."[6] As a finite human being, you'll never be able to fully understand this complex world (or even your own mind!), but you can take hold of the promise that God's peace will guard you like a shield as you walk through the valleys of life.

---

5   1 Corinthians 2:16

6   Philippians 4:7

> ### → Pray
>
> Father, grant me the serenity to accept the things I cannot change, the courage to change the things I can, and the wisdom to know the difference.[7]

# Day 14 Reflections:

**When have you noticed yourself "looking before leaping" and using wise prudence in making decisions?**

**How have you fallen victim to narrow framing or confirmation bias? What about analysis paralysis?**

**What is comforting about the fact that God's peace stands guard over you when making decisions?**

> ### → Respond
>
> Write down a difficult decision you've been pondering. Then answer the question, "What would I tell my best friend to do in this scenario? Oftentimes, you are likely to give more clear and concrete advice to someone other than yourself.

---

7   Serenity Prayer

# Overcoming Suspicion

*The works of his hands are faithful and just; all his precepts are trustworthy.*

—Psalm 111:7

PSYCHOLOGIST PAUL WATZLAWICK SHARED A STORY ABOUT a man who wanted to hang a picture in his home but had no hammer. Remembering that his neighbor has a hammer, the man decides to go and ask to borrow it. But then he thinks to himself, *What if the neighbor won't let me have it? After all, he barely acknowledged my friendly greeting the day before.* He begins to doubt that his neighbor is a kind person at all and starts feeling repulsed by him. He storms over, rings the door bell, and before the neighbor can even say, "Good morning," the man shouts, "You can keep your stupid hammer!"[2]

> If you lead, you will eventually serve with Judas or Peter.
>
> –Dan B. Allender[1]

Though over-the-top, does this story ring true? Have you ever found yourself getting suspicious of others or worked up over nothing? When Sixes are stressed or unhealthy, their natural protectiveness

---

1  Dan B. Allender, *Leading with a Limp: Take Full Advantage of Your Most Powerful Weakness* (United States: Waterbrook Press, Colorado Springs, CO, 2008), 31.

2  Rohr and Ebert, *The Enneagram*, 134.

can turn into paranoia. Webster defines paranoia as "an excessive or irrational suspiciousness and distrustfulness of others."[3]

At times, your suspicions will turn out to be spot-on. For example, the prophet Micah lived in a day when all of Jerusalem's ways seem crooked and relationships feel out of joint. Injustice is running rampant; it seems no one can be trusted. Micah warns, "Put no trust in a neighbor; have no confidence in a friend; guard the doors of your mouth from her who lies in your arms."[4] Like the prophet, you may feel as if everyone seems to be doing what is right in their own eyes, self-serving and untrustworthy.

That being said, Micah's situation was uncommon and it would be burdensome to carry his level of suspicion with you at all times. Paranoid Sixes will always be waiting for the other shoe to drop, and in their most extreme form, they may believe they are being persecuted, singled out, or poisoned by those around them. This line of thinking is not based on facts, but rather from a cynical view of the world that sees most people as dangerous and self-serving.[5]

> Repentance for a Six looks like letting go of unfounded suspicions and choosing to trust.

When Sixes exhibit more phobic behavior, they will deal with suspicion by taking defensive measures. When they exhibit more counterphobic behavior, they will go on the offensive, provoking authority figures with questions and challenges. They think, "How will you deal with me when you see me at my worst? If you remain fair and in control when under attack, then I have some assurance I can trust you and won't be afraid you'll attack me when I've let my guard down."[6]

The growth path for all Sixes is to learn how to regain trust and hold on to faith in people. Enneagram author Sarajane Case advises filtering circumstances, not

---

3   Merriam-Webster.com Dictionary, s.v. "paranoia," accessed October 20, 2021, https://www.merriam-webster.com/dictionary/paranoia.

4   Micah 7:5

5   Sandra Maitri, *The Spiritual Dimension of the Enneagram: Nine Faces of the Soul* (United States: Penguin Publishing Group, 2000), 78.

6   Wagner, *Nine Lenses*, 346.

people. Rather than coming to a concrete conclusion after only just meeting someone, take time and effort to get closer and make an evaluation based on each individual interaction. Furthermore, Case also encourages you to be cautious of running others' kind words and actions through a lie detector. Do your best to receive the compliments and celebrate the qualities they see in you, rather than assuming they must be trying to get something.[7] Ask clarifying questions rather than assuming; go back to that person you are suspicious of and say, "What did you mean by that?"

At the end of the day, as Suzaane Stabile points out, trust is a decision.[8] Repentance for a Six looks like letting go of unfounded suspicions and choosing to trust. Everything we do in life is dependent on the foundation of trust. When Sixes are healthy, they will do the hard work of building trust with their family members, friends, and co-workers. This trust becomes the glue that holds relationships and communities together for the long haul.

***The Good News for Loyalists*** is that God is someone we can trust when the world seems overrun with liars. As the Psalmist proclaimed, "The works of his hands are faithful and just; all his precepts are trustworthy."[9] God not only comforts us with this truth but challenges us as well: "while we were enemies we were reconciled to God."[10] Jesus didn't die for us at our best, but when we were at our worst. This means seeking to build (or rebuild trust) with those we are suspicious of is no longer optional but has become our daily ministry as Christ-followers.[11]

---

7    Sarajane Case, *The Honest Enneagram: Know Your Type, Own Your Challenges, Embrace Your Growth* (United States: Andrews McMeel Publishing, 2020).

8    Stabile, *The Path Between Us*, 160.

9    Psalm 111:7

10    Romans 5:10

11    2 Corinthians 5:19

**→ Pray**

Father, I'm grateful I can count on You. You've never given me a reason not to trust You. Thank You for turning me, an enemy, into Your trusted friend forever. Help me feel the weight of my calling to have a ministry of reconciliation. Empower me today to be someone who puts my suspicions to the test and loves people by assuming the best about them.

# Day 15 Reflections:

**When have you caught yourself being overly paranoid?**

**What types of suspicious activity put others on your "most wanted" list?**

**What unfounded suspicions or unreasonable standards do you need to let go of today? Who do you need to start trusting?**

**→ Respond**

Schedule a conversation with someone you are suspicious of and ask clarifying questions to test your assumptions (lovingly).

# Playing God's Advocate

*For everything there is a season, and a time for every matter under heaven: a*

*time to be born, and a time to die; a time to plant, and a time to pluck up what*

*is planted: a time to kill, and a time to heal; a time to break down, and a time*

*to build up.*

—Ecclesiastes 3:1-3

---

HAVE YOU EVER FOUND YOURSELF PLAYING DEVIL'S advocate in a conversation or group? In our workplaces and churches, it seems that many leaders are given a free pass for their next great idea, which all too often ends in disaster.

Centuries ago, the Catholic Church created a formal position called the *advocatus diaboli* to act as a mitigating, questioning force in the canonization process. This literal "devil's advocate" would seek to discover the truth of a possible saint's character and history to be sure the women and men the church was raising up were worthy of such honor. Though Pope John Paul II

> Cynics always say no ... Saying yes is how things grow.
>
> –Stephen Colbert[1]

---

1   Dave Ferguson and Alan Hirsch, *On the Verge: A Journey Into the Apostolic Future of the Church* (United States: Zondervan, 2011), 218.

eliminated the position in 1983, the popular term is still very much a part of our vocabulary today.[2]

It's unfortunate that this role is often not appreciated in our day. Sixes, who perform this function better than anyone, may be viewed as the villain for doing their duty to provide cross-examination in the courtroom of life. However, without people truly committed to making wise, well-informed decisions, people like me (a dynamic Three) can run too fast toward new ideas, recklessly cutting corners and putting others in danger (literally or metaphorically). I have come to realize—though it's taken some time—that Loyalists are God's advocates, helping me think through the implications of my decisions.

Have you ever thought of doubt as a gift? Helen Palmer says, "Doubt can produce unusual powers of discernment."[3] Your doubts lead you to become a sleuth who looks at the facts, finds inconsistencies, sees holes in arguments, and reveals hidden motives. Doubts disappear with honest questioning, and Sixes love clarity, so they tend to ask a lot of questions to achieve that end.

> Put the exclamation mark of your life's work on what you can plant, building up others as one of God's advocates.

Enneagram teacher Beatrice Chestnut shares that Sixes are diverse—either warm and sensitive questioners, cool intellectual analysts, or hot assertive contrarians. Below the surface though, all Sixes are asking the hard questions: Can this leader be trusted? What threats are visible or hiding from view? What might go wrong? Sixes poke holes in the best-laid plans, looking for the weakest points to either challenge the whole foundation or help their team to patch it up and make it stronger. But once a plan gets off the ground, the questions have only begun! You may feel compelled along the way to keep nudging to make sure the leaders are still trustworthy by following up every action with a debrief session and rehashing old decisions.[4]

---

2    Heath and Heath, *Decisive: How to Make Better Choices.*

3    Helen Palmer, *The Enneagram in Love and Work: Understanding Your Intimate and Business Relationships* (HarperOne, 2010), 159.

4    Chestnut, *The 9 Types of Leadership*, 194-197.

In the wisdom literature of Ecclesiastes, the teacher says there is an appointed time or season for everything under the sun, a time to plant and a time to uproot. My wife Lindsey loves gardening and knows this well: in our backyard, we have six chickens and a few big garden boxes. Every season begins with planting, and every season ends with uprooting. Both are required to get delicious fruits and vegetables on our dinner table.

Likewise, to create and cultivate a healthy family and team, become a gardener, giving yourself to the work of both planting and uprooting. Continue to ask the necessary questions that may uproot half-baked plans, weak theories, and unqualified leaders. But don't forget to plant your concerns with solutions, acknowledging the positives first—so you don't get the reputation for being the wet blanket—and sowing seeds of encouragement.

***The Good News for Loyalists*** is that God is the Master Gardener who not only uproots the weeds of sin in our lives but also plants seeds of truth and encouragement daily. Though it's true that God called the prophet Jeremiah to send a message of dire warning to God's people that they faced possible uprooting, being plucked up if they did not abandon their idolatrous ways, some Bible commentators note that references to building and planting outnumber uprooting and tearing down in these prophecies.[5] Therefore, as someone who reflects the *imago Dei* and seeks the genuine welfare and protection of all, make sure to put the exclamation mark of your life's work on what you can plant, building up others as one of God's advocates—because the devil already has enough.

---

### ➜ Pray

Father, You are the Vinedresser who patiently does the work of planting and uprooting in my life. I cannot bear any fruit apart from You. Help me to abide in Your Son Jesus, the True Vine, and watch closely as the Spirit produces the fruit of righteousness. Because You've given me the task of cultivating, help me to build up others as You have done for me.

---

5   Paul W. Ferris and Michael L. Brown, PhD, *Jeremiah, Lamentations* (United States: Zondervan Academic, 2017).

# Day 16 Reflections:

**Why is playing "devil's advocate" absolutely essential for our health and success?**

**Describe a time when you played "devil's advocate" and it saved a person or group? Have you ever thought of yourself as God's advocate?**

**Is your lead foot planting (affirmation, encouragement, solutions, etc.) or uprooting (testing, raising concerns, constructive feedback, etc.)? What is one thing you can do to plant more?**

## → Respond

Think of someone in the home or workplace you are responsible for. List one piece of constructive feedback and three pieces of encouragement to share with them. Get into the habit of planting more than you uproot.

# Cowardice to Courage

*And I tell you, you are Peter, and on this rock I will build my church, and the*

*gates of hell shall not prevail against it.*

—Matthew 16:18

LOYALISTS ARE STEREOTYPED AS THE MOST FEARFUL personality on the Enneagram, but I find this to be a misunderstanding. In fact, I have found them often to be the most courageous, as their primary vice of anxiety can be transposed into the virtue of courage if given the opportunity. As Dan B. Allender says, "Courage never takes away fear; courage simply redistributes fear to get the job done."

> Courage never takes away fear; courage simply redistributes fear to get the job done.
>
> –Dan B. Allender[1]

Peter was one of Jesus's most loyal disciples. He was one of the first to drop his net and leave everything behind to follow Jesus,[2] he identified Jesus as the

---

1   Allender, *Leading with a Limp,* 77.

2   Matthew 4:18-20

Christ,[3] and he was the first to swear at the Last Supper that he would not betray his Lord, promising, "I am ready to go with you both to prison and to death."[4] But Jesus saw the false bravado under this bold profession: "I tell you, Peter, the rooster will not crow this day, until you deny three times that you know me."[5]

Later that same night, the high priest's servants came to arrest Jesus in the garden. Feeling an overwhelming duty to protect his Lord and forgetting (or ignoring) his Master's prophecies of death, Peter draws his sword and strikes one of the servants, cutting off his ear.[6] But Jesus immediately tells Peter to put away his weapon, promising him that such means were not of the kingdom, having more to do with fear than faith.[7]

After Jesus is hauled away, Peter follows at a distance and tries to find his bearings around a fire in the courtyard. Here, his fear manifests again—this time not through swaggering strength (counterphobic behavior), but deception and hiding (phobic behavior). A servant woman sees Peter sitting in the firelight, recognizes him, and calls him out publicly for being a disciple, but he denies Jesus three times. As Peter hears the rooster crow and remembers Jesus's prediction, he flees and weeps despairingly, having failed the ultimate test.[8]

> Christ's forgiveness gave Peter the courage to neither cower in fear nor lash out with his sword.

Aside from all the disciples' cowardice, another person directly betrayed Jesus that night, only his story ends very differently. Judas, alone at the end with his despair, takes his own life, but Peter is reconciled to his Lord and community. What happened, you ask? Peter remained in his loneliness and pain until Christ returned and drew him in, sharing a meal and affirming, even commissioning

---

3   Matthew 16:15-16

4   Luke 22:33

5   Luke 22:34

6   John 18:10

7   Matthew 26:52

8   Luke 22:55-62

words.[9] Only the enduring love and limitless grace of Jesus could have turned a fearful liar into the courageous, de facto leader of the first century church! Do you believe He can create the same transformation in you?

***The Good News for Loyalists*** is that through Christ, our cowardice is transposed into courage. Even our greatest failing becomes an invitation for a greater experience of loving-kindness. Like Peter, if you have the courage to come back to Jesus after your all too human failings are made known, you will receive tender mercy and hope for a fresh start. Years later, when Peter was ordered by the high council not to speak of Jesus anymore, he boldly declared, "Whether it is right in the sight of God to listen to you rather than to God, you must judge, for we cannot but speak of what we have seen and heard."[10]

Who or what are you running from and need courage to stand up to? Or conversely, what real or perceived enemies do you need to stop taking swings at? Christ's forgiveness gave Peter the courage to neither cower in fear nor lash out with his sword, but rather to exhibit a non-violent resistance like his Savior, who chose radical, self-giving love over hate. According to tradition, Peter was eventually crucified upside down because he didn't feel worthy to die in the same way as his Lord. Did you know that same loving-courage resides within you?

---

### → Pray

Father, You are big and man is small. Forgive me for the ways I allow the fear of others to control my life. Give me courage to keep me from running away and love to keep me from attacking. Empower me by Your Spirit to live from a foundation of faith and not fear. Because Your Son Jesus had the courage to die for me, help me to take a stand today for Him.

---

9   John 21:15-19

10   Acts 4:19-20

# Day 17 Reflections:

**Describe a time you faced your fears with courage.**

**When was the last time you took a stand? Was it rooted in fearful self-protection or faith-filled love?**

**What is so scandalous about the trust Jesus gives Peter to be the leader of the church even after his fall? How does that comfort or challenge you today?**

---

### → Respond

Do that dangerous, difficult, or painful thing you know you need to do but is completely outside of your comfort zone.

# Deep Friendship

*For I desire steadfast love and not sacrifice, the knowledge of God rather than*

*burnt offerings.*

—Hosea 6:6

WHEN I ATTENDED COLLEGE IN THE EARLY 2000s, I was as fashionable as they came: fraternity gear, the visor with spiked hair and frosted tips, puka shell necklace—I was even once mistaken for a Backstreet Boy (just don't ask me to sing like one)! I felt pretty confident in myself. That is, until I started to lose my hair. Finally, on my 30th birthday, I gave in and shaved my head, turning this Nick Carter look-alike into the "bald guy." Funny as it sounds, this was a traumatic experience for an image-conscious Three, but my dear Loyalist Lindsey didn't bat an eye watching my birthday drama unfold, telling me that "Even without hair, you are the most handsome guy in the world."

> [Loyalists] love who you are, not your image.
>
> —Helen Palmer[1]

Silly as all this seems, Lindsey had no idea how much this meant to me. It reminds me of something Helen Palmer says about Loyalists: "They

---

1   Palmer, *The Enneagram in Love and Work*, 167.

love who you are, not your image."[2] This incredible inclination for Sixes to love people for who they are, regardless of status or image, makes you an invaluable gift to anyone who is in a relationship with you. I love that Sixes attach themselves to people over-against personas or utility, going above and beyond your share of responsibility and always putting your loved ones first.[3]

Generally speaking, friendship trumps romance for the Loyalists. In romantic relationships, deep friendship is the highest priority. Riso and Hudson point out that Sixes aren't as sentimental as other types and tend to take a less "rose-colored" view of their relationships (and the world, for that matter).[4] Sixes can be romantic, but they prefer reality over anything that feels artificial. Once they do find and trust someone, their hard-working, responsible nature takes over, often leading them to take on the practical tasks in the relationship from planning the calendar, to running errands, to cleaning the house. Sixes are the opposite of the old adage, "Some people are so heavenly minded that they are of no earthly good."

> Friendship trumps romance for the Loyalists.

Because you are so helpful, it's hard when others don't reciprocate your dedication, but God knows. In the Old Testament, God was frustrated by the lack of depth in His relationship with the Israelites. Though their feasts, festivals, and sacrifices were abundant, they utterly failed to pursue justice, mercy, and humility.[5] Jesus similarly called down the religious leaders in His day, claiming they had "neglected the weightier matters of the law: justice and mercy and faithfulness."[6] Similarly, it may be heartbreaking when your partner or friend does the same thing to you—outwardly offer kind pleasantries or romantic gestures from time to time—but you sense their loyalty lies elsewhere.

***The Good News for Loyalists*** is that in Jesus we have the perfect friend—committed, responsible, hardworking, and forgiving. He "shows no partiality"[7]

---

2   Ibid., 167.

3   Palmer, *The Enneagram in Love and Work*, 165-166.

4   Riso and Hudson, *Personality Types*, 223.

5   Micah 6:6-8

6   Matthew 23:23

7   Romans 2:11

and invites all to come to Him regardless of whatever special or fabricated image we present to the world. Jesus died on the cross—not for our social media-sculpted self—but our flawed and ordinary selves lying behind the lens. Jesus spent time with ordinary men and women who weren't impressive in the eyes of the world—the lepers, paralytics, tax collectors, prostitutes, and those struggling with mental health, not offering divine dictums from on high, but serving amid a lost and shepherdless people in pain.

Paul even recognized this aspect of what it means to be truly human in Jesus's example: "who, though he was in the form of God, did not regard equality with God as something to be exploited, but emptied himself, taking the form of a slave, being born in human likeness."[8] Walk in these holy footsteps proudly as a Six, embodying the same kind of fidelity and servanthood Jesus did in befriending and serving all people.

---

### → Pray

Father, thank You for being my eternal Friend. You walked and talked with Adam and Eve, called Abraham Your friend, spoke to Moses face to face, and sent Your Son Jesus to come into the world as a friend of sinners. In a world filled with relationships lacking commitment, use me to display your fidelity and offer forgiveness to those who don't give it back.

---

8   Philippians 2:6-7 NRSV

# Day 18 Reflections:

**How has a significant other or friend shown great commitment to you?**

**Who do you need to let go of because your loyalty isn't being reciprocated anymore?**

**What do you appreciate most about the way Jesus sees and expresses friendship?**

---

**→ Respond**

Choose one relationship you currently have and write out what you'd like it to become. How do you want it to feel? What kinds of things do you do for each other? Then sit down with that person and communicate your desires.

# Blind Spots in Love

*Love is patient and kind; love does not envy or boast; it is not arrogant or rude. It does not insist on its own way; it is not irritable or resentful; it does not rejoice at wrongdoing, but rejoices with the truth. Love bears all things, believes all things, hopes all things, endures all things.*

—*1 Corinthians 13:4-7*

THE FIRST TIME WE SIT BEHIND THE wheel of a car, we discover that what we can't see may hurt us. The safest way to drive is to practice constant awareness, minding our vehicle's blind spots and attending to the flow and rhythm of traffic. The same is true when navigating relationships: our failure to see the needs of those with whom we live and work can lead to unintentional pain for all. Yesterday, we looked at some of the healthy qualities of a Loyalist in relationships; today, we are going to take a hard but necessary look at some of the blind spots Sixes must be aware of when they move toward unhealthiness.

One of the challenges for some Loyalists is creating a healthy balance between dependence and

> Love is giving someone the power to destroy you but trusting them not to.
>
> –Unknown

independence. For example, Sixes derive a sense of safety and security from time spent with their relationships. But, there's a limit. If Sixes find themselves around immature or needy people, they will unconsciously swing toward independence. Furthermore, due to the broad range of variability in Sixes, responses to individual and relational unhealth can run the gamut from completely independent to deeply codependent. For example, a more phobic Six may desire independence from their parents so strongly they run off and become dependent on a controlling partner, or they may decide to stay in a codependent relationship simply because they fear being without support.[1] Meanwhile, other Sixes may become overly dependent on authority figures, peer groups, parents, or a set of rules to maintain clear boundaries in their life.

One place in Scripture that talks about blind spots is the apostle Paul's classic chapter on love in 1 Corinthians. Paul starts by telling us love is patient. When Sixes are unhealthy, their doubts and insecurities lead them to become impatient and annoyed if they don't receive daily reassurances. As a result, they may demand to stay in close physical contact or repeatedly ask, *Do you still want to be with me?*

> You are the fun, steady, loyal best friend we so desperately need.

Next we learn that love is not irritable. The great thing about Sixes is they will engage conflict out of a true desire to preserve the relationship. The only caveat is that when Sixes are unhealthy they become reactionary—wearing their irritability on their sleeve, playing the blame-game, and asking accusatory questions. Enneagram author Drew Moser describes this result as being like sandpaper, "which, overused, can eventually stop smoothing and actually wear something down."[2]

Then Paul says love believes all things. While Sixes have a seemingly endless ability to "bear all things," take note that Paul also encourages you to remain positive. Rather than continually questioning your loved one's intentions or

---

1  Riso and Hudson, *The Wisdom*, 245.

2  Moser, *The Enneagram of Discernment*, 279..

harboring suspicions, divine love gives us the power to truly believe the best about them. Trust their motives unless they give you a hard and fast reason not to!

These blind spots aren't fun to hear, so let me remind you that you are a rock for the relationships around you. You are the fun, steady, loyal best friend we so desperately need. Your grit and "staying power" is the glue that holds us together. Your crazy generosity is seen by all. As one Six shared, "If you give me a steak, I will return to you a cow."[3] You are our strong ally, our devoted supporter, and when we are with you we know we can take on the world together!

***The Good News for Loyalists*** is that in the light of Jesus's life of sacrificial love, we can see our blind spots clearly. Through Jesus, the multi-faceted love of the Triune Godhead described in 1 Corinthians 13 has been made visible to us. Just as a diverse spectrum of bright colors shine through a crystal prism, so too does the patience, kindness, truth, and enduring love of the Father shine through the Son with magnificent glory. If you have seen and tasted this radiant love, you ought to go and love others in the same way today.

---

## → Pray

Father, You are love itself. When it comes to being patient and trusting, my love sometimes falls incredibly short. Help me think the best about others as You think the best about me. Enable me by Your Holy Spirit to demonstrate hope and kindness from the well of Your steadfast love which endures forever.

---

3  Ian Morgan Cron and Suzanne Stabile, *The Road Back to You Study Guide* (United States: InterVarsity Press, 2016), 47.

# Day 19 Reflections:

**What situations cause you to run toward independence and/or dependence?**

**How does not being able to fully predict what someone else will do enhance rather than diminish love?**

**How have you grown in being patient, easygoing, and trusting in your relationships? Which area would you like to see growth in?**

---

### → Respond

When we begin a relationship, it's easy to see the other person's great qualities. However, over time we may begin to take them for granted. Choose a relationship that's valuable to you, identify two to three strengths in that relationship, and share memories that illustrate them.[4]

---

4  This exercise comes from www.therapistaid.com.

# Grieving with Hope

*But we do not want you to be uninformed, brothers, about those who are asleep,*

*that you may not grieve as others do who have no hope.*

—1 Thessalonians 4:13

"Jesus wept."[1] Those words repeated through my lowered head as I sat at my desk, my own tears welling up. A long road of infertility had rocked my marriage, leaving crushed dreams and hopes deferred. Experiences like this are difficult for anyone, but when the ones from whom you seek comfort grieve differently, it can add alienation and loneliness to the pain.

> Wrestling with God is a sign of intimacy. You can't wrestle with someone you're far away from.
>
> —Jon Acuff

For years, my wife cried and cried, unable to believe we'd ever see a miracle, and to this day, still no miracle. I, on the other hand, didn't cry but instead kept telling her to have faith. Looking back, I can see now that what I had was not faith but naivety (and that telling anyone struggling to simply have faith is never

---

1   John 11:35

a good call). I suppressed my emotions by naively assuming everything would work out, but this was just an unconscious strategy to sweep things under the rug. In so doing, I suppressed Lindsey's pain, dodged her emotions, failed to offer God's presence, and held fast to stoicism when I should have been sowing tears.

Thankfully, we joined a small group of believers who felt stuck in various ways. During one of our sessions, the leader pointed his finger at me and sternly said, "David was a man who grieved and was called a man after God's own heart. You haven't done that." Those stern words shocked me out of passivity, and the next morning, as I sat reading the story of Lazarus, I finally broke open. Coming across the powerfully short line, "Jesus wept," I heard God tell me: "Lindsey's tears are My tears." And for the first time since we began our struggle, I too wept.

The apostle Paul tells the Thessalonian church that his desire for them is to grieve with hope. Do you struggle like me with the grieving part? To find the courage to face your unfulfilled longings? Or do you identify more with Lindsey, who is able to grieve but struggles at times to cultivate hope?

> You can bring every concern to Jesus without fear of being rejected.

At times, it can seem like the Bible is contradictory. Jesus told His disciples, "Therefore I tell you, whatever you ask in prayer, believe that you have received it, and it will be yours."[2] Lindsey and I shake our heads as we witness so many surprise pregnancies—and all the while, we are on our knees in prayer. Is God's Word not true? It would be a lot easier for all of us, especially for you as a Loyalist, to just do what God expects and know your prayers will be answered in return. This "do good, get good" mentality is a major theme in the book of Proverbs, but "do good, get good" is about probabilities not absolutes. God in His sovereignty can choose to make exceptions to the rule to serve a higher purpose, one that we often cannot see.

Unanswered prayers litter the pages of Scripture. Paul prays for God to take away his "thorn … in the flesh," but continues to suffer.[3] Lazarus's sisters ask

---

2   Mark 11:24

3   2 Corinthians 12:7-12

Jesus to come right away, but He doesn't.[4] A story Lindsey and I resonate with is Zechariah and Elizabeth's, as they also struggled with infertility. They were "advanced in years," which means they experienced heartache for a very long time.[5] They must've been confused about God's silence; after all, they were "walking blamelessly in all the commandments and statutes of the Lord."[6]

***The Good News for Loyalists*** is you can bring every concern to Jesus without fear of being rejected. Grieving doesn't look like naively believing everything will work out, but it doesn't look like going through life stoically ignoring the pain either. It's about both shedding tears and clinging to the promise that "those who sow in tears shall reap with shouts of joy!"[7] Though the Bible is filled with righteous saints with unfulfilled longings on an individual level, it's clear that God's purposes are always fulfilled for His people. Therefore, just as Zechariah and Elizabeth continued to serve God faithfully while they patiently waited, resist the temptation to fall into despair and self-pity. Instead, grieve with hope along with the saints of old, who longed for the fulfilment of God's promises and "saw them from a distance" and "greeted them."[8]

---

### → Pray

Father, I've often felt confused by my circumstances and sometimes ignored. Give me the courage to pour out my concerns to You with brutal honesty rather than fall into resentment. I know You can take it. Empower me by Your Spirit to carry the burden of unanswered prayers and trust that You'll come through for me even if it's in a way I couldn't foresee.

---

4   John 11:1-4

5   Luke 1:7

6   Luke 1:6

7   Psalm 126:5

8   Hebrews 11:13 CSB

# Day 20 Reflections:

**Was "wrestling with God" encouraged or discouraged in your church growing up? What about now?**

**What unanswered prayer has been the hardest for you to carry and why?**

**What feelings or false narratives do you need to let go of so you can grieve with hope?**

> ### → Respond
>
> Write out your own prayer of lament using Psalm 22. What are you feeling (vv. 1-2)? What has been the most difficult part of the struggle? What do you want the Lord to do (vv. 19-21)? What praises will you proclaim (vv. 22-31)?

# A Porcupine's Projection

*What causes quarrels and what causes fights among you? Is it not this, that*

*your passions are at war within you?*

—James 4:1

---

THE NINETEENTH CENTURY PHILOSOPHER ARTHUR SCHOPENHAUER CAME up with a parable popularly known as "the Hedgehog's Dilemma." This story about the desire for intimacy and its challenges describes a situation in which a group of porcupines seek to get close to one another to share their body heat during a very cold winter. However, due to their sharp quills, they must keep their distance to avoid poking each other. They desperately need close physical contact with one another, but they will inevitably get hurt.[2]

> The best political, social, and spiritual work we can do is to withdraw the projection of our shadow onto others.
>
> –Carl Jung[1]

This parable illustrates the Loyalist's inner-struggle to have physical

---

1   Scilla Elworthy, *Pioneering the Possible: Awakened Leadership for a World That Works* (United States: North Atlantic Books, 2014).

2   Walter Veit, "The Hedgehog's Dilemma," Psychology Today (Sussex Publishers, March 28, 2020), https://www.psychologytoday.com/us/blog/science-and-philosophy/202003/the-hedgehog-s-dilemma.

and emotional intimacy with the keen awareness that pain is almost inevitable. Thus, Sixes often cope with a defense mechanism—not unlike a porcupine's quills—called projection. *Projection* is "attributing to others motives, feelings, or thoughts not acknowledged in oneself."[3] Drew Moser puts it this way: "Sixes see their internal issues as belonging to external forces."[4] Contrast this with introjection, the Type Four defense mechanism, which causes an internalization of criticism, leading them to turn against themselves.

When Sixes feel something is off within, they may look for external clues to explain their anxiety. This can play out in a variety of ways: You might feel unsettled because you believe a co-worker or other relationship has an expectation of you they haven't expressed. Or, if you are angry with an authority figure, you might project onto them that they are actually mad at you. You might also imagine someone is judging you if you are feeling insecure about yourself. And, if you are feeling guilty and want to clear yourself of any alleged fault, you might blame someone else. A very unhealthy Six's past will be littered with a long list of scapegoats who they've sent off into the wilderness with their sins.

> Projection is not protection, but a defense mechanism that turns friends into enemies.

When your own internal fears, doubts, and mistrust become a weight that feels impossible to lift, you will be tempted to take weight off your own bar and put it on someone else's bench press. Projection is a survival tactic to disown, get rid of, and offload the inner anxiety, but it ultimately leads to loneliness and a defensiveness toward everyone in your life.

When you feel your suspicions toward others increase, the apostle James challenges you to look within first—to figure out if it's really another's quills or yours that are causing the issue. He asks, "What causes quarrels and what causes fights among you? Is it not this, that your passions are at war within you?"[5] Though our enmity with others often looks ugly and horrific on the

---

3   Claudio Naranjo, *Character and Neurosis: An Integrative View* (United States: Gateways/IDHHB, 1994), 219.

4   Moser, *The Enneagram of Discernment*, 238.

5   James 4:1

outside, James points out that it all starts with an internal, invisible war within our own hearts.

Therefore, before you think you know what someone else is really thinking, ask yourself: "Is this something I intuitively know or something I am projecting?"[6] Examine all the evidence as objectively as you can and ask others you trust to weigh in on the situation if you feel stuck. Try inhabiting the other person's story; how might they explain the situation? Follow the wisdom of Proverbs that exhorts you not to "lean on your own understanding,"[7] but allow God to exchange those false narratives with true ones. As the apostle Paul advises, "take captive every thought to make it obedient to Christ."[8]

***The Good News for Loyalists*** is the battle against anxiety is already won. You've been given the "sword of the Spirit"[9] to fight off the lingering lies that disrupt your internal peace and threaten all of your existing relationships. Rather than making other people the target, which is the accuser's tactic for you, remember that your struggle is not against flesh and blood, but against "the father of lies."[10] Remember, projection is not protection, but a defense mechanism that turns friends into enemies. Relax those quills today and experience the gift of friendship, connection, and intimacy that God gave you to thrive.

---

### → Pray

Father, I praise You that there is "now no condemnation for those who are in Christ Jesus."[11] I don't have to be afraid of looking at what's going on within my heart. Help me to catch myself when I start projecting my anxieties on others. Help me to take every thought captive and experience the joy and intimacy You've given me in all my relationships.

---

6    Chestnut, *The Complete Enneagram*, 218.

7    Proverbs 3:5

8    2 Corinthians 10:5 NIV

9    Ephesians 6:17

10    John 8:44

11    Romans 8:1

# Day 21 Reflections:

**Where do you see evidence of projection in your life?**

**What are you trying to avoid through projecting (guilt, self-condemnation, vulnerability, accountability, responsibility, etc.)?**

**How will seeing yourself through God's non-judgmental eyes give you confidence to look inward the next time you experience angst?**

---

### → Respond

Jot down an expectation (or negative view) you think someone has of you that they haven't verbally expressed. How will you take that thought captive?

# Peace! Be Still!

*And he awoke and rebuked the wind and said to the sea, "Peace! Be still!" And the wind ceased, and there was a great calm. He said to them, "Why are you so afraid? Have you still no faith?"*

—Mark 4:39-40

DO YOU SOMETIMES FEEL AS IF YOU are suffering from perpetual low-grade anxiety? One Loyalist puts their struggle this way: "Anxiety feels like a freight train. It's as if I am standing on a platform, looking down the track. I can feel the train's vibration and feel it coming and then find myself completely taken up by it and can't get off."[2] Can you relate? Are you afraid that "the light at the end of the tunnel" may really just be another train? Does even the concept of worry, well, worry you? You may worry about how much you are worrying, whether you are worrying about the

> Anxiety is like a rocking chair. It gives you something to do, but it doesn't get you very far.
>
> –Jodi Picoult[1]

---

1  Vancil, *Self to Lose Self to Find*, 106.

2  Ibid., 109.

right things, or worry when things are going well because obviously something is wrong if they are.

The primary emotion for those in the Head Triad (Fives, Sixes, and Sevens) is fear. While Fives react to their fear by withdrawing, Sevens distract themselves through constant activity, but Sixes respond in relationship—either turning to others for security (phobic) or against them (counterphobic). Though different Sixes respond in varied ways to their fears, the common denominator is that they all battle anxiety.

This particular blind spot has serious long-term implications as prolonged anxiety can lead to depression, paranoia, feelings of inferiority, panic attacks, constant fear of abandonment, impulsively swinging between dependence and defiance, extreme suspiciousness, attachments to abusive relationships, or lashing out at perceived enemies.[3]

> The God of Peace lives within us, transforming worrying fault finders into hope dealers.

If left unattended, anxiety creates trauma that will wreak havoc in our physical, mental, and spiritual lives for years to come. As Sarajane Case explains, "When we worry, we live through the hard things twice. The experience of stressing over potential trauma can often sit in our bodies as if the trauma were real. Therefore, when we focus our attention on what could go wrong, we live through the experience whether or not we end up having to actually live through it."[4]

The growth path for Sixes means integrating the healthy characteristics of a Type Nine. When this happens, the Six becomes peaceful, emotionally stable, receptive, open-minded, and sympathetic. They will take on the gentleness, kindness, child-like optimism, and overall sunny disposition that often characterizes Nines.[5] The inclination to worry isn't banished, but it is kept at bay.

One day a storm came along and threatened the lives of Jesus and His disciples. As the disciples (many lifelong sailors) struggle against the wind and waves, Jesus

---

3   Riso and Hudson, *The Wisdom*, 253.

4   Sarajane Case, *The Honest Enneagram*, 154.

5   Riso and Hudson, *Personality Types*, 253-254.

is taking a peaceful nap. The terrified men wake Him up and shout, "Teacher, do you not care that we are perishing?"[6] We learn so much about the disciples' assumptions from just this one powerful question: They assume they are going to die—which, given that many grew up on the water, may have been correct. They assume Jesus doesn't care—why else would He simply leave them to deal with the buffeted boat? And they assume Jesus has no power over the frightening storm. As this is still early in His ministry, they have no reason to suspect Jesus can do what He does—in fact, their first response is to wonder: *Who is this man?* Nevertheless, He rebukes their lack of faith after commanding the storm: "Peace! Be Still!"[7]

Imagine for a moment if the disciples would have acted in *faith* rather than fear. What if Jesus would have woken to a group of hopeful men who knew they would receive help if they only asked?

***The Good News for Loyalists*** is that the Spirit of the God of Peace lives within us, transforming worrying fault finders into hope dealers.[8] Because you are a temple of the Holy Spirit, take your eyes off the wind and waves swirling around and look within. There you will find the Spirit of Jesus, giving you the power to speak with authority over your stormy soul, "Peace! Be Still!" My prayer is the same prayer Paul spoke over his beloved churches in Rome: "May the God of hope fill you with all joy and peace in believing, so that by the power of the Holy Spirit you may abound in hope."[9]

---

### ➜ Pray

Father, there is not one square inch of creation that falls outside Your sovereign control. Forgive me for the assumptions I've made about You when things aren't going my way. I will not let tomorrow's worries steal today's peace. Transform me into a calm, reassuring son or daughter who strengthens the body of Christ with hope when the storms come.

---

6    Mark 4:38

7    Mark 4:39

8    Craig Groeschel, "My Big Fat Mouth - Criticizing," LifeChurch, 2021, https://www.life.church/media/my-big-fat-mouth/criticizing/.

9    Romans 15:13

# Day 22 Reflections:

**When has prolonged anxiety led you down a dark path? How did God guide you out of that season?**

**What are three or more areas of your life where fear, anxiety, or doubt keep showing up? What assumptions might be increasing your level of anxiety?**

**How does the story of Jesus calming the storm give you hope and assurance to face the next storm?**

---

**➡ Respond**

Talk to a mentor or spiritual director this week about the areas of life where fear and anxiety keep showing up.

Day 23:

# Stress Triggers

And Moses lifted up his hand and struck the rock with his staff twice, and water came out abundantly, and the congregation drank, and their livestock. And the LORD said to Moses and Aaron, "Because you did not believe in me, to uphold me as holy in the eyes of the people of Israel, therefore you shall not bring this assembly into the land that I have given them."

—Numbers 20:11-12

WE ALL GET STRESSED FROM TIME TO time, but if we don't pay attention to the warning signs, we will find ourselves at the breaking point quickly—or maybe even in a public meltdown. Beth McCord shares some of the most common triggers for the Loyalist that may lead to a blow up:

- feeling targeted, blamed, or accused unfairly

> No pressure, no diamonds.
>
> –Thomas Carlyle[1]

- feeling put under undue pressure

- believing others are not being genuine, authentic, and honest

---

1   Iam A. Freeman, *Seeds of Revolution: A Collection of Axioms, Passages and Proverbs, Volume 1* (United Kingdom: iUniverse, 2014), 74.

- seeing others' lack of commitment, loyalty, and follow-through

- being or feeling lied to or abandoned

- believing others do not take your anxieties or concerns seriously[2]

Because conflict threatens relational security, one of the Loyalist's greatest strengths is a desire to bring truths out into the open right away to protect the relationship. Again, this occurs in divergent ways: whereas Phobic Sixes need space to think things through, Counterphobic Sixes describe a readiness to engage. Sometimes, the Six's emotional realness may annoy their loved one if they become too reactive, or their focus is more on problems than solutions.[3] Inwardly, a Six may be feeling anxious, but others may experience this anxiety as free-floating angst.

> Because God has a long fuse, He doesn't react, retaliate, or punish quickly, but is merciful and forbearing.

Anxiety can cause a build-up that eventually leads to a blow-up. One Six shares how he experienced this at work one day: "What can I do? I can't do it by myself, and I can't count on anyone else to help get this moving. This is such important work, and yet no one seems to care about it but me. My boss told me to get this done within six months and to find the resources to do it, but there's nothing available. I almost feel like this is a setup, but why would anyone want me to fail?"[4]

The Bible presents many case studies of people who shut down completely or lashed out in a public meltdown because of stress. One of those whose failures were very visible (and came with steep consequences) is Moses. More than once, he seems to throw up his hands, telling God he would rather die than deal with the unfaithful Israelites another moment. While the shutdowns often occur in

---

2    Jeff and Beth McCord, *Becoming Us: Using the Enneagram to Create a Thriving Gospel-Centered Marriage* (United States: Morgan James Publishing, 2019), 144.

3    Kacie Berghoef and Melanie Bell, *The Modern Enneagram: Discover Who You Are and Who You Can Be* (United States: Callisto Media Incorporated, 2017), 131.

4    Ginger Lapid-Bogda Ph.D., *Bringing Out the Best in Everyone You Coach: Use the Enneagram System for Exceptional Results* (United States: McGraw-Hill Education, 2009).

private, Moses's public meltdowns take place before the entire nation—like the one at Meribah, when he strikes the rock.[5]

Moses had a very stressful job—in the hot desert for over forty years, no less!—so it's understandable that he sometimes bends past the breaking point. He listens to constant complaining, bickering, and backsliding and is somehow supposed to always know what to do. Not only that, but his leadership and authority are under constant threat by his own friends and family. We hear often of Moses's self-doubt, frustration, loneliness, and anger, and his final public failure at Meribah is the stated reason he is denied entry to the promised land. Nonetheless, Moses always recovers and stands with his people, faithfully leading them to the doorstep of Canaan.

***The Good News for Loyalists*** is that there is a way to bend without breaking. You are loved by a God who is "merciful and gracious, slow to anger and abounding in steadfast love and faithfulness."[6] He is long-suffering toward us which means He suffers a long time before showing anger. Because He has a long fuse, He doesn't react, retaliate, or punish quickly, but is merciful and forbearing. Likewise, God is ready and willing to give you a longer fuse so you can act honorably before all and "uphold [God] as holy in the eyes of the people"[7]—the very thing Moses failed to do at Meribah.

Let your stress lead to sanctification—a cleansing. Just as Jesus received the world's hostility on the cross and yet reverberated love in a remarkable demonstration of self-control, you too can pour out grace on even the most unfair and careless people you know.

---

5   Numbers 20:10-13

6   Psalm 86:15

7   Numbers 20:12

### → Pray

Father, thank You for sending Your Son to be our example of someone who bent without breaking. Through temptation, opposition, persecution, and even death, He did not fold. Oh Lord, let the same compassion flow out of me that flowed out of Jesus when He was struck on the cross. With Your steadfast patience, I will point my friends and enemies to the promised land of a life lived with You today.

# Day 23 Reflections:

**What triggers your stress most often? What past stressful experiences might actually be diagnosed as trauma?**

_______________________________________________

_______________________________________________

_______________________________________________

_______________________________________________

**How has your emotional realness been misunderstood as a challenge rather than a desire to preserve the relationship?**

_______________________________________________

_______________________________________________

_______________________________________________

_______________________________________________

**What steps can you take now to prevent a public meltdown like the one Moses experienced?**

_______________________________________________

_______________________________________________

_______________________________________________

### → Respond

Because others may be able to see the warning signs before you do, ask someone to share how they can tell when you are stressed out.

# Thriving at Work

*Then I said to them, "You see the trouble we are in, how Jerusalem lies in ruins with its gates burned. Come, let us build the wall of Jerusalem, that we may no longer suffer derision."*

—Nehemiah 2:17

"JUST PRAY ABOUT IT." THESE WERE THE words I shared with my best friend in college after he came to my dorm room for some much-needed advice. Has anyone ever told you that? While it's true that prayer is absolutely essential, I know now that telling someone to "let go and let God" is generally unhelpful and often causes more harm than good. Nehemiah, the fifth century BC leader who supervised the rebuilding of Jerusalem was more of a practical God-follower.

> God isn't offended by your biggest dreams or boldest prayers. He is offended by anything less.
>
> –Mark Batterson[1]

After hearing that Jerusalem's walls were broken down and its gates destroyed by fire, he sat down and wept for days—praying and fasting.

---

1 Mark Batterson, *The Circle Maker: Praying Circles Around Your Biggest Dreams and Greatest Fears* (United States: Zondervan, 2016).

This city was the symbol of his people, the City of David, where heaven met earth in God's temple. So, rather than waiting for God to send someone else, Nehemiah realizes God wants him to be the answer to his own prayer. He travels to Jerusalem, secretly surveys the rubble, and determines the size and scope of the project before committing to it. Then, to everyone's surprise, this cup-bearer is able to get permission to rebuild from the king of their captors, Artaxerxes. Not only that, but the king even donates supplies for the massive project and offers a military escort.[2]

Similarly, Sixes have the same incredible work ethic displayed by Nehemiah. They are honest, humble, quick-witted, and courageous leaders. They typically don't like the spotlight, but give credit to others. Sixes will caution when their team is headed down the wrong track, call out the higher-ups when needed, ask the tough questions, creatively solve problems, write contingency plans, and keep everyone safe.[3] Sixes share that they are often drawn to problem-solving fields such as academia, legal professions, law enforcement, banking, administration, and health care.

> Healthy Sixes do not let problem-solving turn into problem-seeking.

However, just like everyone, Sixes have a few work pet-peeves. Beatrice Chestnut teaches that they don't enjoy it when others tell them "not to worry" or become flaky or unreliable; they hate vague instructions or expectations, the misuse of power, or prioritizing speed over careful analysis. Furthermore, they also get peeved when others pressure them to make quick decisions, don't take their concerns seriously, don't care about processes or due diligence, or view them as negative or pessimistic.[4]

While many of these frustrations are valid, co-workers of unhealthy Sixes have shared that they can be hard to work for a number of reasons: they can ask too many questions, waver in indecision, make things overly-complicated, give too

---

2  Nehemiah 1:3–2:8

3  Chestnut, *The 9 Types of Leadership*, 210.

4  Ibid., 206-208.

much information, don't trust their colleagues, project a cynical attitude, or express so much skepticism that it undermines the team's confidence.[5]

However, when Sixes are healthy, they can thrive in the workplace when they clarify their intentions, moderate contrarian reactivity, focus on what could go right, learn to trust others, and do not let problem-solving turn into problem-seeking. Another helpful suggestion from Chestnut is for Sixes to express concerns behind the scene with their direct report before bringing them up in team meetings.[6]

Because Sixes are responsible and tend to take on the bulk of the tasks, they can easily become stressed out and overwhelmed. Therefore, another helpful tip for you is to delegate more and break down all your tasks into bite-sized steps. Lastly, make sure to get away from your workspace often to clear your busy mind by taking walks, gardening, cooking, or doing something physically active.

***The Good News for Loyalists*** is though your labor in the home or workplace can be toilsome and frustrating, you'll be able to look back like Nehemiah and say, "for the good hand of my God was upon me."[7] The work Nehemiah set out to do appeared outrageous, unrealistic, and dangerous and was threatened by corruption and malicious neighbors. And yet God used Nehemiah to do more than the Jews could ask or imagine during a time of despairing captivity. Working in the King's court, Nehemiah could have settled for compliance, but instead pursued courage. Whatever challenges you are facing at work today, don't just "pray about it," but lean confidently into your practical gifts to accomplish more than you or anyone else thinks is possible.

---

5   Ibid., 210-211.

6   Ibid., 219-220.

7   Nehemiah 2:8

> ### → Pray
>
> Father, forgive me for settling for compliance when Your desire is that I'd lead out with courage. You said that if we ask anything in Your name You'll give it to us.[8] Therefore, help me pray bigger, bolder prayers as I dream about best-case scenarios. Because you've given me incredible practical gifts, use me today to be the answer to someone else's prayer.

# Day 24 Reflections:

**What are your top work pet peeves?**

_______________________________________________

_______________________________________________

_______________________________________________

_______________________________________________

**How would you like to become a healthier team player?**

_______________________________________________

_______________________________________________

_______________________________________________

**What seemingly impossible project would you like to accomplish if you knew God's hand was upon you?**

_______________________________________________

_______________________________________________

_______________________________________________

> ### → Respond
>
> Get out a piece of paper or digital device and do a brain-dump. Write down all your fears, worries, or stressors. You'll notice that using this technique will help you feel less overwhelmed simply by clearing your mind.

8   John 16:23

# Dealing with Doubt

*And have mercy on those who doubt.*

—Jude 1:22

LINDSEY AND I LOVE WATCHING HOME IMPROVEMENT shows. There's just something so satisfying about watching an old house's dignity be restored. It's inspiring to see a condemned building in a new light as house-flippers walk through and talk about its amazing potential. What if we approached our faith journey in the same way? Though our past or present religious experience doesn't look pretty, what if we could look into the future and see potential?

The number of "exvangelicals" is growing—those who are walking away from this expression of the faith and leaving a condemned sign on the door. Have you been disillusioned by the hypocrisy and infighting, the racism and power-hunger, the abuse and affairs, and celebrity-culture in the church? There's a lot to shake our heads about and I'm sure you've wondered: *Is there a way to honestly face our doubts, deconstruct our faith, and critique the church without walking away from Jesus in the process?*

> Doubt is not the opposite of faith; it is one element of faith.
>
> —Paul Tillich

While God's Word—Christ—is the "solid rock" of the house that we live in, it's important to point out that our faith tradition, culture, or family have done a lot of decorating before we came along. Are you mad about the wallpaper or appalled by the extra room that was added on without a safety permit? Are you frustrated by the lack of maintenance and disheartened by those kitchen countertops that are in poor taste and represent a culture we'd rather forget?

In the end, these are not poor reflections of God, but of the renters. In your understandable frustration, do not think you must tear down the whole structure all together—after all, every house has it's issues. Rather, like a wise house-flipper, we must do the hard work of figuring out what needs to go and what needs to stay; what is in accordance with the person of Christ and what is man-made. Perhaps the conservative wallpaper in the parlor that others have claimed has been there forever needs to go, or maybe the new progressive paint palette that makes us feel enlightened when we walk in doesn't facilitate the right mood after all.

> Like a wise house-flipper, we must do the hard work of figuring out what needs to go and what needs to stay.

House-flipping is just as legitimate as Jesus's table-flipping. When Jesus saw that the new money-making wing of the Temple did not belong there, He had no problems with scheduling a demo day. Along these lines, it's important to note that Jesus wasn't afraid to flip tables in the Jewish tradition He grew up in. You might be the kind of Six who has put too much trust in your tradition. If you are tempted to never question your spiritual authorities or feel as if your church is the best church, the next step for you today might be to open the aperture of your spiritual lens to take a wider look. Maybe you need to find a new community or tradition or show grace to those who already have. Maybe there's work to do in those rooms whose doors you always keep closed.

***The Good News for Loyalists*** is God engages those who doubt—indeed, doubting is a vital part of a growing faith.[1] When the disciple Thomas proclaims, "Unless I see in his hands the mark of the nails, and place my finger into the

---

1  Jude 1:22

mark of the nails, and place my hand into his side, I will never believe," Jesus engages His friend.[2]

Perhaps you are like Thomas, who needed hands-on experience, or like Jacob, who had to literally wrestle with God to move on.[3] Perhaps you are the Prodigal Son, who left his home to find a better one, but returns with a new appreciation of all he once rejected.[4] If you are in a figurative "distant land" today, filled with doubt or skepticism, know the Father is waiting for you to return home and fall into His loving arms. Some of us must leave to return. Some of us must leave and make a life elsewhere. Either way, the Father will meet us where we are. Wherever you are, be an agent of change and help remodel your faith community—because all houses need to be flipped from time to time. When the foundation is good, we can always bring new life.

---

**→ Pray**

Father, help my unbelief! Enable me to come through my doubts with stronger and deeper roots than before. Forgive me for the times I've blamed You or the church when, in reality, my real angst was toward fake Christianity. Fill me with Your Spirit and reconstruct my faith experience in a way that allows me to heal the local church rather than criticize it.

---

2   John 20:25-28

3   Genesis 32:22-32

4   Luke 15:11-32

# Day 25 Reflections:

**What questions do you have for God?**

**What teaching or current reality in the church causes you to doubt? Is it a timeless truth or cultural additive you are truly wrestling with? Explain.**

**To what extent does your local church allow its members to doubt? How can you help your church "have mercy on those who doubt?"**

> ## → Respond
>
> Set up a meeting with a mentor or mature group of people to process the hard topics such as sex, race, politics, social justice, science, hell, and the like.

# Social Security

*[Elijah] said, "I have been very jealous for the LORD, the God of hosts. For the people of Israel have forsaken your covenant, thrown down your altars, and killed your prophets with the sword, and I, even I only, am left, and they seek my life, to take it away."*

—1 Kings 19:10

---

HAVE YOU EVER FELT ALONE AND WITHOUT support? Meet the prophet Elijah. The wicked rulers of Israel, King Ahab and Queen Jezebel oversaw a land brimming with immorality, religious and social corruption, and pagan worship. Elijah's fierce loyalty to the Lord gives him the courage to host a showdown between the God of Israel and the prophets of Baal on Mount Carmel where, in a supernatural display of divine power, the Lord shows Himself victorious over the false gods. After Elijah has the false prophets seized and put to death, I'm sure he feels like he is finally going to get the spiritual revival he's been waiting for.[2]

> **Real security can only be found in that which can never be taken from you.**
> –Rick Warren[1]

---

1   Rick Warren, *The Purpose Driven Life: What On Earth Am I Here For?* (United States: Zondervan, 2011).

2   1 Kings 18

Only, revival doesn't come, and Elijah soon finds himself on the run from a queen Jezebel who publicly issues a death warrant. After he's run all the way to Mount Horeb, he sits alone in a cave feeling hopeless and abandoned. The Lord's prophet then grieves: "For the people of Israel have forsaken your covenant, thrown down your altars, and killed your prophets with the sword, and I, even I only, am left, and they seek my life, to take it away."[3]

According to Beth McCord, a Loyalist's core fears include "feeling fear itself, being without support, security, or guidance; and being blamed, targeted, alone, or physically abandoned."[4] Therefore, Sixes may seek out social security through a belief system, friend group, military, counselor, mentor, or partner. Stephanie Hall Barron adds that "Sixes often find a partner who is calm where they are anxious, and bold where they are fearful."[5] Sixes will then find themselves looking for outside guidance and support, searching for that sure foundation they can depend upon for the security they crave. That's why they will make sacrifices and invest time and energy into reinforcing their support system, seeking reassurance from authorities, and checking in with their allies to make sure they are still "on their side."[6]

> Jesus invites you to stop basing your personal well-being and safety in others and instead find it in Him.

The growth path for a Six involves recognizing the limitations of over-relying on others as a security net. If you realize you've attached yourself to the wrong person or group it may be too late to get out, which leaves you feeling more alone and vulnerable than before. In behavioral economics, this is called "consumer lock-in" or the "sunk-cost fallacy." Once you've invested a high level of time, energy, and resources into one relationship or group, you're much less likely to "get out" and change to another option.[7] Once this happens, a Six may slide to the unhealthy side of Type Threes

---

3   1 Kings 19:10

4   McCord, *Becoming Us*, 144.

5   Stephanie Barron Hall, *The Enneagram in Love: A Roadmap for Building and Strengthening Romantic Relationships* (United States: Rockridge Press, 2020), 61.

6   Riso and Hudson, *The Wisdom*, 243.

7   Meg Jay, "The Downside of Cohabiting before Marriage," The New York Times (The New York Times, April 14, 2012), https://www.nytimes.com/2012/04/15/opinion/sunday/the-downside-of-cohabiting-before-marriage.html.

and worry about how they look to others, change to "acceptable" jargon, and do whatever it takes to avoid rejection.

But Jesus offers another way. He invites you to stop basing your personal well-being and safety in others and instead find it in Him. If your identity is based on shifting things like relationships, groups, or a specific set of ideals, you can soon find your peace swept away with what remains after others have failed you.

***The Good News for Loyalists*** is that when we trust in Christ, building our lives on His solidity and finding our identity securely hidden within Him, He becomes both our solid rock and tower of refuge. Overidentifying with others will cause you to sacrifice your desires, needs, and interests, but when you merge with Jesus, He provides a secure path to become more of who you were meant to be.

When Elijah flees into the wilderness, feeling alone and wanting to die, God sends an angel to put food and water by his head. Shortly after, at Mount Horeb, Elijah expresses the grief-filled fear that he is now God's lone loyal follower, but the Divine voice speaks to him in a gentle whisper, revealing that there are still seven thousand in Israel who have not bowed their knees to Baal.[8] Today, let this story be a reminder that you are not alone or abandoned. Even when you can't see it or feel it, God is still there!

---

### → Pray

Father, I will sing with the psalmist, "You are my LORD; I have no good apart from you."[9] Open my eyes to see the countless ways You've supported me. Forgive me for seeking my security and well-being in relationships, social networks, and the ideals they stand for. You are my solid rock and in You alone I can finally become the person You made me to be.

---

8    1 Kings 19:18

9    Psalm 16:2

# Day 26 Reflections:

**When have you felt all alone, without support, blamed, targeted, or abandoned?**

**What social security systems have you been clinging to for support? What would you do or who would you be if these were taken from you?**

**What needs, desires, beliefs, or interests of yours differ from those of your support systems? Which of those might Jesus be calling you to take a stand on?**

---

## → Respond

Create a list of all the ways God is supporting you right now: family members who've given you financial support, unknown factory workers who made your clothes, the utility workers who keep your electricity on, and so on.[10]

---

10  Riso and Hudson, *The Wisdom*, 257.

# Be Prepared

*Afterward the other virgins came also, saying, "Lord, lord, open to us." But he answered, "Truly, I say to you, I do not know you." Watch therefore, for you know neither the day nor the hour.*

—Matthew 25:11-13

JESUS ONCE SHARED A STORY ABOUT THE importance of preparation called the parable of the ten virgins. In the first century, a wedding ceremony included a procession through the streets after nightfall to the groom's home. These ten virgins in Jesus's parable were young bridesmaids, expected to carry their own torch as they waited for and followed the groom in the wedding procession.

> There's no harm in hoping for the best as long as you're prepared for the worst.
> —Stephen King[1]

As the story goes, the groom is a "long time in coming," and five of the young women are adequately prepared with enough oil for their torches to last the night, but the other five are not. As midnight rolls around, the ten

---

1  Cron and Stabile, *The Road Back to You*, 189.

women are awakened by the sound of the groom's approach. However, the five unprepared bridesmaids wake to find their torches out and, though they beg for oil from the others, they are told to go buy their own. While they are away, the groom arrives, the marriage feast begins, and the front door is locked. When the women return, they are refused access to the feast.[2] Though this parable is primarily about remaining vigilant for Christ's return, we also learn a timeless principle from Jesus: the wise are prepared, but the foolish pay the price for their lack of planning.

One of the hallmark features of a Loyalist is being prepared. The motto of a Six is the same as the Coast Guard: *Semper Paratus* (Latin for "Always Ready"), and they've likely memorized the verse: "Be sober-minded; be watchful. Your adversary the devil prowls around like a roaring lion, seeking someone to devour."[3]

> Don't allow anxiety to become a safe place for you because you believe more worrying will lead to more security.

When going on trips, Sixes will keep a checklist and be ready for every contingency. The vehicle's oil will be changed, the spare tire is filled, and emergency snacks and water bottles are stowed away. One of the many reasons we love you is your ability to think ahead and keep us safe. As a Three, I'll spend all my time thinking about what could go right, which is great until everything falls apart, like that oil change I forgot about from Day 4—or the bridesmaids in Jesus's parable.

Your job—a calling, even—is to help your loved ones and team think through their decisions and plan for every outcome. With your patience and discipline, we can be *saved* from getting into debt, hiring the wrong person, losing others' trust, damaging our reputation, forgetting to maintain our assets, and in some cases, from injury or loss of life. You are a divine gift of safety and security to those you're in relationship with.

---

2   Matthew 25:1-13

3   1 Peter 5:8

**The Good News for Loyalists** is that the burden of preparedness doesn't all fall on you. You can't and shouldn't be expected to carry that weight. Because we serve an omniscient God, you don't have to wear yourself out thinking about every possible traumatic situation. The Bible reminds us, "[God] knows everything,"[4] and "Even before a word is on my tongue, behold, O Lord, you know it altogether."[5] Your job is to work your magic of planning and then let go. Being more prepared won't always keep you from danger because you can't control every outcome. Life is filled with curve balls, so don't allow anxiety to become a safe place for you because you believe more worrying will lead to more security. Instead, spend time preparing in proportion to the task at hand, saving the rest of your God-given energy for self-care and living life to the fullest.

---

## → Pray

Father, I will cast my burdens on You, for You will sustain me and not let me be moved.[6] Thank You for giving me the gift of preparation to guard myself and others from evil and the painful consequences of hasty decisions. Help me to discern when I'm crossing the line from preparedness into anxiety. I will trust You to establish all of my steps and keep me secure.

---

4   1 John 3:20

5   Psalm 139:4

6   Psalm 55:22

# Day 27 Reflections:

**Describe a significant event in which your preparation paid off.**

**What is within your power to secure and what is beyond your ability (or responsibility)?**

**What would change if you truly believed God is prepared for every outcome?**

---

### → Respond

Plan a mock disaster (health emergency, losing your children at the store, assault or abuse charges, etc.) and gather your family or staff team together to involve everyone in creating a preparation checklist.

# Structure Submits To Spirit

*I am the vine; you are the branches. Whoever abides in me and I in him, he it is*

*that bears much fruit, for apart from me you can do nothing.*

—John 15:5

---

IN *THE TRELLIS AND THE VINE*, AUTHORS Tony Payne and Colin Marshall compare a church's ministry structures to a trellis—wooden, fence-like structures made to support and display vine-growing plants. Payne and Marshall argue that while building the trellis is a necessary first step, the primary goal of ministry is to grow the vine (the people making up the kingdom), not the trellis. The structures exist to support and extend the true work of ministry, which is being Christ—the living Word of God—to one another. Their big idea is that "structures don't grow ministry any more than trellises grow vines."

> Structures don't grow ministry any more than trellises grow vines.
> —Tony Payne and Colin Marshall[1]

Structures and systems have a very important place in our families, churches, and almost any other organization—formal and informal alike. As mentioned, a vine

---

1  Tony Payne and Colin Marshall, *The Trellis and the Vine: The Ministry Mind-shift that Changes Everything* (Austria: Matthias Media, 2009).

cannot grow without the support of a trellis, but Loyalists must avoid the pitfall of becoming overly-reliant on these structures to provide spiritual growth and forward progress. Jesus said that apart from abiding in Him, the Vine, our hard work on the systems and structures will all be for nothing.

Loyalists tend to build structure into their lives to exchange anxiety and ambivalence for stability and continuity.[2] While others often feel oppressed by rigorous structures, Sixes feel safer and more secure in them. Sixes feel strengthened operating within well-defined procedures and guidelines, but when someone from the outside rocks the boat by introducing change, it can be frightening if their personal identity is wrapped up in those things.

Annabelle, a therapist, explains why change is so difficult: "I am a creature of habit and routine. You see, each time I deliberately create a habit, I have one less thing to think about. Otherwise, I would use that much more energy thinking. I hate change. I have a knee-jerk negative reaction to change. Change means that the future will be different. The good news is that I'll adjust as soon as the future gets predictable again or as soon as I get one of my systems or explanations into place."[3] The path of growth for the Loyalist, then, is to make these adjustments quicker. My friend Adam, a pastor and Enneagram coach (who is himself a Loyalist), says, "[We] need to learn how to pivot." Jesus wasn't very predictable and kept His disciples on their toes His entire ministry; His "School of Discipleship" wasn't a consistent nine-to-five job with weekends off—life with Him was more like sailing than jumping onto a cruise ship with an itinerary.

> Structures were made for man, not man for structures.

Sailing is an activity that requires complete dependence on the wind (the Greek word for "wind," *pneuma*, is the same used for spirit). Just as a trellis is necessary for a vine to grow, we must set the sails to catch the wind of the Holy Spirit. If we don't do the vital work of preparation, we won't be ready when the Spirit moves. However, greater dedication to the plan than to the Spirit is like overly-taut sails—the wind cannot adequately fill them, and you'll go nowhere. Sixes

---

2  Riso and Hudson, *Personality Types*, 219.

3  Riso and Hudson, *The Wisdom*, 247.

must learn to pivot or "go with the flow" (like Type Nines, which is where Sixes go in health) and surrender their best-laid plans to the guidance of the Spirit.

**The Good News for Loyalists** is, Paul reminds us, God provides the growth,[4] so the pressure is off—we must build our trellises as securely as we know how and let the divine Vinegrower do His work.[5] Remember, structures (including those we believe to be scripturally-sound) were made for man, not man for structures. Keep trimming those sails, remaining aware of the *pneuma* piloting your course, so you are ready to pivot and move where it leads.

### → Pray

Father, no matter who waters or who plants, You cause the growth. Help me not to become so busy building the trellis that I forget to spend time abiding in You. Thank You for giving me the gift of building healthy structures to support kingdom work. I will trust Your Spirit over my plans and remain available and flexible for whatever You have next.

---

4   1 Corinthians 3:6

5   John 15:1-11

# Day 28 Reflections:

**How has your trellis work supported the growth of your family, church, or workplace?**

**Are you spending more time cultivating the vine or building the trellis?**

**How does the gospel free you to become more flexible and hold your plans more loosely?**

---

**→ Respond**

Mark off a day on your calendar to go somewhere new—ironically, plan to be spontaneous. Don't decide ahead what you'll do or prepare anything in advance. Just go with the flow and enjoy the wind filling your sails.

*Day 29:*

# The Watchman

*Unless the LORD watches over the city, the watchman stays awake in vain. It is in vain that you rise up early and go late to rest, eating the bread of anxious toil; for he gives to his beloved sleep.*

—Psalm 127:1b-2

UNTIL I BECAME A PASTOR, I WAS naive about what went on behind the scenes in a church. Now, though I want to worship on Sundays free from care, I realize part of my calling as a shepherd (and a parent) is to remain vigilant. I've encountered many people in my time who have or would bring harm to those under my care, so I have been pushed quite strongly along the growth path toward the protective and cautious mind of a Six.

I think of Loyalists as God's Secret Service: they are vigilant, natural risk assessors, always reading people to search for hidden agendas or ulterior motives. They know where the exits are in any room and what's standing in the way between them and the door. Like a radar, they constantly scan their environment, picking up potential

> Go to sleep in peace.
>
> God is awake.
>
> –Victor Hugo[1]

---

1   Victor Hugo, *The Letters of Victor Hugo* (United States: Houghton, 1898).

dangers that others may never see. Like zebras on a savanna, they maintain just the right distance from their predators—never close enough to get caught by the lions, yet never so far away they lose visual contact.[2]

Throughout the Bible, we read of watchmen: people whose sole duty was to sit at the gate, walk the city, or patrol upon the walls, keeping their eyes open for danger. Though a guarded city would employ watchmen all day, the night was the time of greatest risk; therefore, greater vigilance was required. Nights were divided into three "watches," consisting of four hours each, and while on duty, the watchers must push through the weariness of staring into the darkness. If they fell asleep, a fire could break out or an enemy attack. These watchmen took their jobs very seriously, and I bet a few of them even went above and beyond, practicing extreme measures of caution to make themselves and others feel more at peace. Yet in the end, King Solomon warns that "unless the LORD watches over the city, the watchman stays awake in vain."[3] In other words: it doesn't matter how long they stand guard or how much they exhaust themselves over extra safety measures, the reality is that unless the Lord is watching, no one is truly safe.

> Submitting to the Lord means resting in security, neither worrying over tomorrow nor replaying today.

Do you feel like you are always "on duty," never able to fully relax for fear of something catastrophic happening? Would you like for someone to relieve you of duty so you can fully accept the gift of divine rest? Would you like to get through this devotion today without thinking about that "thing" you can't stop worrying about?

***The Good News for Loyalists*** is the Lord gives rest to the weary: "for he gives to his beloved sleep."[4] As David sings in the fourth Psalm, "In peace I will both lie down and sleep; for you alone, O LORD, make me dwell in safety."[5] God is your

---

2    Wagner, *Nine Lenses*, 346-347.

3    Psalm 127:1

4    Psalm 127:2

5    Psalm 4:8

Watchman, standing guard over you, offering to exchange your anxiety for rest. He doesn't want (or expect) you to "be on" 24/7. Part of submitting to the Lord means resting in security, neither worrying over tomorrow nor replaying today, but accepting His continued mercies. He stands waiting for you when the night watch is over and the dawn breaks.

### → Pray

Father, I praise You because You have called me beloved. I will gladly receive your invitation to rest today. Along with the apostle Paul, in my watchfulness, I will give thanks and devote myself to prayer.[6] Remind me that being on guard at all times will only feed my anxiety and lead to exhaustion, but allowing You to be my Watchman will leave me satisfied.

---

6   Colossians 4:2

# Day 29 Reflections:

**What are the majority of your thoughts focused on when you lay in bed at night?**

**Describe a time when you were able to go "off duty" and be fully present with God or others. What led you to feel at rest?**

**What would your life be like if you let go of the deistic belief that God is disengaged and expects you to fend for yourself?**

---

**→ Respond**

Look up the popular hymn "Great is Thy Faithfulness." Meditate on the lyrics or lay down and listen to the song remembering God's faithfulness toward you.

# The Good/Bad Split

*And God saw everything that he had made, and behold, it was very good.*

—Genesis 1:31

A LOYALIST'S NATURAL TENDENCY IS TO BISECT the world into "good" and "bad," separating nearly everything into mutually-exclusive binaries. This is called *splitting*, and it is the second primary defense mechanism of the Six.[2] This instinctive practice is an attempt to extend control and therefore lessen anxiety's hold, but the result is almost always negative. You'll be amazed how often you naturally put your own self or preferences in the "good" category, while dismissing those you don't trust or understand into the "bad."

> The line dividing good and evil cuts through the heart of every human being.
>
> –Aleksandr Solzhenitsyn[1]

A few of these "splitting" behaviors include quickly passing judgment on others before getting to know them, treating the leaders we trust as special or powerful, cutting people out of your life or lashing out once they

---

1   Daniel J. Mahoney, *Aleksandr Solzhenitsyn: The Ascent from Ideology* (United Kingdom: Rowman & Littlefield Publishers, 2001), 50.

2   Chestnut, *The Complete Enneagram*, 191-192.

"cross the line," or expecting others to "choose sides," either agreeing with you or aligning with "Them."[3]

The perceived benefit of splitting is that it helps your psyche cope with life's uncertainties. Life feels safer when you know who the "good guys" and the "bad guys" are. Another perceived benefit is that once you are able to locate the "badness," you can then distance yourself from it—an immoral leader, tainted theology, wayward church, or an unbiblical political party—of course, your leader, theology, church, or party is the "good" one. Doing the good/bad split is why unhealthy Sixes tend to have either friends or enemies—there's no room for grey. As Helen Palmer says, unhealthy Sixes will either be "at your feet or at your throat."[4]

But what happens when you find the "badness" within your own self or chosen team? What happens when an issue or person simply refuses to be categorized? This can cause you to spiral and even reject everything you once subconsciously saw as "good"—including yourself.[5] This is where the defense mechanism will fail: either leaving you fighting against yourself or projecting fear, confusion, and anger onto someone else. This is why Sixes must come to terms with the fact that good and evil will always coexist in the world—including within yourself.

> Love chooses progress over perfection.

When God created the world and everything in it, He said over and over again that it was "good."[6] Not soon after, the enemy slithers into the lives of Adam and Eve, seeking to kill and destroy the love and trust between Creator and creation. After tasting the forbidden fruit, Adam and Eve hide in shame, separating themselves (badness) from their Creator (goodness). When God pursues, Adam attempts to blame Eve, who likewise blames the serpent. Yet, under this attempt

---

3   Rebecca Ogle, "How to Deal with Splitting Behavior - the Wellness Society: Self-Help, Therapy and Coaching Tools," The Wellness Society | Self-Help, Therapy and Coaching Tools, June 4, 2021, https://thewellnesssociety.org/how-to-deal-with-splitting-behavior/.

4   Palmer, *The Enneagram in Love and Work*, 168.

5   Chestnut, *The Complete Enneagram*, 191-192.

6   Genesis 1

to project their sin onto someone else and keep the badness away, the truth remains: their hearts are "desperately sick."[7]

***The Good News for Loyalists*** is that God mercifully pursues Adam and Eve and replaces their fragile, self-protective fig leaves with better garments. He provides an animal sacrifice to "cover" their perceived badness with His goodness, crossing the divide they believed existed between their hearts and His. Many years later, God would again make the sacrifice to cover the badness of the entire world, showing once for all that we could never adequately cover ourselves or run from the pursuit of divine love.

Thankfully, though good and bad still coexist within each one of us, God doesn't fall into splitting, withdrawing from us when our badness surfaces. Instead, like a skillful painter, He makes use of the many beautiful shades of grey in the world; like a surgeon, He operates gently and precisely on us with truth and grace. Because He treats you this way, You ought to be just as gentle with yourself and others, practicing loving acceptance. Love chooses progress over perfection. As one in whom there is now no condemnation, you ought to withhold judgment, searching for the image of God in all people and allowing God to cover the distance in our hearts.

---

**→ Pray**

Father, I praise You for covering me with Your goodness. Forgive me for attempting to put people into my good and bad boxes. Help me to be kind and compassionate toward those I disagree with or disapprove of, forgiving them just as You have forgiven me.[8] Give me the ability to have a both/and approach to life that sees beauty in the places and people I least expect.

---

7   Jeremiah 17:9

8   Ephesians 4:32

# Day 30 Reflections:

When have you lovingly pursued someone even though there was much disagreement or disapproval?

What are some ways you've done the good/bad split? How has this kept you from acknowledging goodness in all things?

How does focusing on progress over perfection help us love ourselves and others more?

---

**→ Respond**

To work on not polarizing, choose a world religion or political party different from your own and list three perspectives or practices that you can affirm as good.

*Day 31:*

# Success over Survival

*Have I not commanded you? Be strong and courageous. Do not be frightened,*

*and do not be dismayed, for the LORD your God is with you wherever you go.*

—Joshua 1:9

IMMEDIATELY FOLLOWING GOD'S GREAT VICTORY OVER THE Egyptians, the Israelites find themselves standing on the border of Canaan. They are eager to enjoy the "good life" after four centuries of horrific slavery in Egypt in the place promised to their ancestors: a gorgeous land, flowing with milk and honey—their inheritance. But after Moses sends out twelve spies, only ten of the twelve report that the current inhabitants are "giants" and their cities are heavily fortified. The spies conclude that it would be foolish to go up against these foes who make them feel as small as grasshoppers. So against the better judgment of their leaders, the people reject God's promise of success and cowardly retreat into the desert, where they spend the next forty years wandering.[2]

> **Doubt kills more dreams than failure ever will.**
> —Suzy Kassem[1]

---

1   Bill Clark, *Random Reflections From An Everyday Sinner* (United States: Elm Hill, 2019), 78.

2   Numbers 13

Generally-speaking, Loyalists tend to fight for survival more than they do success. They are very talented at identifying and eliminating threats, but often leave their own dreams unfulfilled because success feels like walking into a trap. That's why things actually working out feels so foreign to a Six, almost like a set-up—leaving you exposed to the "giants" in the land.[3]

When Sixes focus primarily on survival, they may manufacture extra responsibilities or otherwise "go around" success by passing off the baton for others to go the distance. As Suzanne Stabile points out, a survival mentality may cause Sixes to become "thinking-repressed": although their minds are always going, productive thinking gets repressed—the kind that moves you from thinking to doing.[4] Just as a person driving around a cul-de-sac for hours may feel like they are headed somewhere, a Six might be deceived into believing their constant thinking is taking them somewhere. But thinking about something is not the same as actually doing it.

> Sixes often leave their own dreams unfulfilled because success feels like walking into a trap.

When Sixes are healthy, they aren't afraid to leave the security of their homes, like Abraham and Sarah, and forge new and adventurous paths. They are willing to partner with those who will help them go the distance, like Moses and Aaron, knowing their legacy will not be determined by what they dream but by what they do. This isn't a path you must walk alone. One of the world's greatest dreamers, Walt Disney, was rather shy and doubted his abilities. On his own, he may have never shared his wonderful creations with the world, but Walt was able to do what he did because of his older, business-savvy brother, Roy. Just as God paired Roy with Walt and Aaron with Moses, God will also put the right people around you to succeed.

***The Good News for Loyalists*** is as the saying goes, "If God brings you to it; He will get you through it." When the Israelites find themselves once again at the doorstep of Canaan, the Lord says to Joshua, "Be strong and courageous ... being careful to do according to all the law that Moses my servant commanded you ...

---

3    Palmer, *The Enneagram in Love and Work*, 160.

4    Stabile, *The Path Between Us*, 155.

that you may have good success wherever you go."[5] After sending out spies again, this time the report comes back that the long-feared "giants" are afraid of them! They advance to Jericho, carry the ark around the walls of the city for six days, and on the seventh day march around seven times before giving a war cry and watching the walls fall down.

Though Jericho wasn't a large city—rather, just a few city blocks—this small but significant win at the entrance to the promised land would give them all the courage they needed to advance toward larger enemies. In the same way, God will provide you with a series of small wins to give you the faith to face bigger obstacles. Therefore, be strong and courageous and pursue the success that is already guaranteed as you obey God's call. Have no fear: The giants standing in your way look like grasshoppers to God. Don't spend the next forty years of your life like the Israelites, circling around the desert, avoiding faith-filled risks. Rather, keep advancing. As Henry Cloud says, "Avoidance of risk is the greatest risk of all."[6]

---

### → Pray

Father, remind me today that playing it safe is too risky. With You there are no risks, for everything You ask me to do is part of Your perfectly thought-out plan. As someone who is drawn to safety, free me to be a risk-taker like Jesus who risked it all on the cross to accomplish Your will and secure a better future for us all. Give me confidence today to face my giants.

---

5  Joshua 1:6-7

6  Henry Cloud, *9 Things You Simply Must Do to Succeed in Love and Life: a Psychologist Probes the Mystery of Why Some Lives Really Work and Others Don't* (Nashville, TN: Thomas Nelson, 2004), 36-37.

# Day 31 Reflections:

**What blessings are you experiencing right now that are a result of someone else taking a risk?**

**What's the worst thing that could happen if you succeeded beyond your expectations? What's the best thing that could happen?**

**What fears, doubts, or obstacles regarding your dreams do you need to surrender to the Lord and trust Him with?**

> **➜ Respond**
>
> Write a fifty-word personal mission statement that will help you prioritize your future pursuits.

*Day 32:*

# Helpless in the Fire

*Shadrach, Meshach, and Abednego answered and said to the king, "O*

*Nebuchadnezzar, we have no need to answer you in this matter. If this be so,*

*our God whom we serve is able to deliver us from the burning fiery furnace,*

*and he will deliver us out of your hand, O king."*

—Daniel 3:16-17

SIX CENTURIES BEFORE THE BIRTH OF CHRIST, Nebuchadnezzar, king of the powerful Babylonian Empire, besieged and conquered Jerusalem, deporting many of their citizens to Babylon—including the young noblemen Shadrach, Meshach, and Abednego. After some time in the king's court, during which they distinguished themselves as men of wisdom and temperance, they became embroiled in the Emperor's ill-fated choice to set up a golden statue for his people to worship. Because they refuse to bow down, they are summoned to the king to answer for their

> Suffering can refine us rather than destroy us because God himself walks with us in the fire.
>
> –Timothy Keller[1]

---

1   Timothy Keller, *Walking with God Through Pain and Suffering* (United States: Penguin Publishing Group, 2015), 9.

insubordination, and they respond by saying, "O Nebuchadnezzar, we have no need to answer you in this matter. If this be so, our God whom we serve is able to deliver us from the burning fiery furnace, and he will deliver us out of your hand, O king."[2] Absolutely furious, Nebuchadnezzar has them tied up and cast into the flames.

A core fear for Loyalists is being helpless or defenseless, so they do whatever they can to keep from being caught off guard, surprised, disappointed, hurt, or betrayed.[3] Determined not to be as helpless as these young men before the king, Sixes throw up defenses, creating a protective outer shell. However, while this defensive position will stop you from experiencing much (though not all) of the pain life sends your way, it will also stop you from experiencing much of its joy.

On a vacation to San Francisco, my wife and I hopped in a rental car and traveled north to Muir Woods, a large redwood forest where some of the trees reach 250 feet high and 30 feet in diameter! Many of these trees were just sprouting seeds when Jesus walked the earth two thousand years ago; it's hard to imagine every one of those towering trees starting as a tiny seed.

> A core fear for Loyalists is being helpless or defenseless.

For an acorn to become a tree, it first has to die by going into the ground and shedding it's protective seed coat. You too must shed your self-protective shell if you want to receive life-giving water and be supported in the nurturing soil of a community.[4] Famously, redwoods do not have deep roots; rather than extending deep underground, they grow outward, intermingling with the rest of the forest, each strengthening the next. To reach your full potential, you first must become as vulnerable as a newborn baby. You must send your roots out, opening yourself to connection—to joy and pain. The Christ-life is one of risk and radical love, arms spread wide in cruciform openness.

***The Good News for Loyalists*** is your fiery trials will refine, not consume you. After King Nebuchadnezzar looks into the furnace, he is astonished, saying, "But

---

2   Daniel 3:16-17

3   Wagner, *Nine Lenses*, 357.

4   Seed metaphor is from Vancil, *Self to Lose Self to Find*, 14.

I see four men unbound, walking in the midst of the fire, and they are not hurt; and the appearance of the fourth is like a son of the gods."[5] As they are pulled out of the fire unharmed, the King declares, "Blessed be the God of Shadrach, Meshach, and Abednego, who has sent his angel and delivered his servants."[6] We learn these three men were miraculously delivered by an angel with an appearance like a "a son of the gods"—they were not alone.

God does not promise a life free of trials, but He does promise to stand with us. As the apostle James said, "Count it all joy, my brothers, when you meet trials of various kinds, for you know that the testing of your faith produces steadfastness. And let steadfastness have its full effect, that you may be perfect and complete, lacking in nothing."[7] Don't be alarmed when life heats up, as it is the fire that purifies us into the people of God.

---

**→ Pray**

Father, I praise You for being a God who shows up in furnaces, jail cells, and colosseums when your people are in danger. Help me learn to be content in fiery trials, for when I am helpless I know I am strong.[8] Allow the flames I experience to refine me rather than consume me. I will let down my defenses today and allow more of Your love to come in.

---

5   Daniel 3:25

6   Daniel 3:28

7   James 1:2-4

8   2 Corinthians 12:10

# Day 32 Reflections:

**Is your faith measured by difficult circumstances or changed character? Explain.**

**How do you put up your defenses when feeling powerless? Have these strategies hurt or helped you?**

**When have you experienced intimacy and growth in a relationship after letting your guard down?**

---

**→ Respond**

Tell a story or share a memory from your past that makes you feel happy. One way to let your guard down is to share something that makes your heart glad.

# Clothed with Power

*"And behold, I am sending the promise of my Father upon you. But stay in the city until you are clothed with power from on high."*

—Luke 24:49

WE LIVE IN A PANDEMIC OF POWER grabs. Worldly power is exerted upon us every day by individuals, corporations, agencies, and yes, religious institutions who seek to use, manipulate, or dominate us for their own ends. As a result of these abuses, it's not surprising that many of us assume all use of power is corrupt.

> [Power] is what enables us to make things happen or not.
>
> –Richard Gula[1]

The Bible talks a lot about the source and use of power. Jesus tells His disciples, "But you will receive power when the Holy Spirit has come upon you …,"[2] while the apostle Paul reminds the Corinthian church that "the kingdom of God does not consist in talk but in power."[3] By the power of the Holy Spirit,

---

1 Richard M. Gula, *Just Ministry: Professional Ethics for Pastoral Ministers* (United States: Paulist Press, 2010), 123.

2 Acts 1:8

3 1 Corinthians 4:20

Jesus is miraculously conceived, is anointed for ministry, heals and teaches others, battles temptations, and is raised to life.

A Jesus-follower is one who is "clothed with power from on high"[4] and does not shy away from using that power, but underdeveloped Loyalists tend to deflect authority, projecting it onto others instead of walking in it themselves. However, once they finally become comfortable with the power they've been given, they overcome their fear and anxiety and grow in self-confidence, finally rejecting the myth that some people are born to lead and others aren't.

You have way more power than you realize. Peter Scazzero, in his book *The Emotionally Healthy Leader*, describes the different sources of our authority: Positional power derives from a title or role we carry, cultural power is based on our age, gender, ethnicity, and privilege.

> Jesus displayed a different kind of power that was submissive, humble, and noncoercive.

Personal power stems from our gifts, knowledge, and education. Projected power is put on us by others. Relational power comes from people entrusting their fears and secrets to us. And "God-factor" power ultimately comes from the sacred authority we've been given by God as stewards of creation.[5] Scazzero's big idea is this: whether or not we are technically "in charge" in all of these spaces, we have more power than we think. He goes on to explain why it's absolutely essential for you to think about these categories and take inventory of your given-authority.

> In my years of teaching and mentoring leaders, I've seen just as much damage result from … leaders who are ambivalent and uncomfortable with their power. Perhaps it's because I identify with them. For these leaders, it somehow feels wrong and unbiblical to grab the reins and take charge because power implies privilege, a higher social status, being above others. The thought of having power as a leader sounds detached and cold. So they prefer to deny or minimize the very real power they have. Some may even feel unworthy or afraid to exercise power,

---

4   Luke 24:49

5   Scazzero, *The Emotionally Healthy Leader*, 245-247.

especially in God's name. As a result, they live in a fog, feeling powerless internally, yet responsible to exercise power to lead others.[6]

Rather than ignoring or giving away your power, you must assert your authority in the power of the Holy Spirit to both maximize your service to others and protect them from power-hungry leaders. Scazzero points out that when we are reluctant to exercise our power, we open the door for the wrong people to assert themselves and cause harm in our circles of influence.

***The Good News for Loyalists*** is that we've been given the good gift of power with the ability to steward it in the right time, in the right way, and for the right purposes. Jesus used His divine authority to disarm all forms of worldly power through His death and resurrection, triumphing over them in victory.[7] He displayed a different kind of power that was submissive, humble, and noncoercive, exercising it under the authority of His Father—setting aside His status and privileges—and selflessly serving the good of all.[8] Following Jesus's example and walking in the power of the Holy Spirit, put on an unshakable self-confidence today, knowing you have what it takes to to stand your ground, make tough decisions on your own, and do more than you think you are capable of. God gave you "a spirit not of fear but of power and love and self-control."[9]

---

### → Pray

Father, oh the immeasurable greatness of Your power toward us who believe![10] I praise Your Son Jesus for being crucified in weakness so I would be able to live by the power of God with Him forever.[11] Help me not to shy away from the power You've given me but steward it to serve and protect others.

---

6   Ibid., 243.

7   Colossians 2:15

8   John 12:49-50, Philippians 2:6, Luke 17:12-19, John 4:7-26

9   2 Timothy 1:7

10   Ephesians 1:19

11   2 Corinthians 13:4

# Day 33 Reflections:

**When have you witnessed leaders abusing power? Has this frightened you from stepping into bigger roles?**

**How did Jesus manifest His power?**

**What more good in the world could you do if you were given more power?**

---

## → Respond

Name your sources of power using Scazzero's help: What formal positions do you hold? What gifts, skills, and assets has God given you? What people or groups have given you permission to speak into their lives? What power do you have based on your age, ethnicity, gender, or other cultural factors?[12]

---

12   Scazzero, *The Emotionally Healthy Leader*, 248.

# Words Matter

*Death and life are in the power of the tongue, and those who love it will eat*

*its fruits.*

—Proverbs 18:21

THE GREAT CHICAGO FIRE IN 1871 LEFT 100,000 people homeless, 17,000 buildings destroyed, 300 people dead, and 40 million dollars' worth of damage done. Though never confirmed, legend holds that the fire started when the O'Leary family's cow knocked over a lantern, setting the city's largely wooden infrastructure ablaze.[1] One principle from this story remains: one spark can set the world on fire. The apostle James connects the potential power of our words to a spark too: "So also the tongue is a small member, yet it boasts of great things. How great a forest is set ablaze by such a small fire!"[2]

> Words matter, and the right words matter most of all. In the end, they're all that remain of us.
>
> –John Birmingham

---

1   History.com Editors, "Chicago Fire of 1871," History.com (A&E Television Networks, March 4, 2010), https://www.history.com/topics/19th-century/great-chicago-fire.

2   James 3:5

Loyalists' tongues are more flammable than most; an unhealthy one may start fires through grumbling, complaining, victimizing, or blaming. As we talked about in Day 21, the defense mechanism of projection allows Sixes to escape their inner anxiety by projecting their angst onto others—allowing the belief that others cause their uncomfortable feelings. They may find themselves saying things like "You made me lose my temper," or "If you hadn't done/said …, I wouldn't have had to say what I did." Sometimes though, Sixes may reserve the harshest words for themselves if they think they were too irresponsible or unprepared.

Once you realize you've gone too far with your words, there are three practical steps we can all take: You can start by confessing any negativity you might have put "into the air" through your anger or sarcasm.

Next, we must learn to be quick to *forgive* others. Suzanne Stabile shares that it's hard for the average Six to "forgive and forget" because they believe they can better protect themselves by remembering past disappointments. Forgiveness is tough because it can make a Six feel vulnerable and powerless, but in the end, refusing forgiveness keeps you in chains more than anyone else.[3] But there is healing available if you let go of your past and bring your pain to Jesus, who knows exactly what it feels like to be criticized, betrayed, or taken advantage of.

> Be a coach and not a critic.

Sixes should also seek to encourage: "Let no corrupting talk come out of your mouths, but only such as is good for building up, as fits the occasion, that it may give grace to those who hear."[4] In other words, be a coach and not a critic. A critic focuses on what you did wrong; a coach focuses on what you can do right. When you criticize someone, even when it's done constructively, you are making a "withdrawal." And if you make more withdrawals than deposits, over time the relationship will end up in the negative—which translates to increased stress and more resentment. A coach, however, seeks to build up relational equality rather than deplete it, which leaves more than enough trust for those times you need to give constructive feedback.

---

3   Stabile, *The Path Between Us*, 159.

4   Ephesians 4:29

***The Good News for Loyalists*** is that Proverbs says life, not just death, is found in the power of the tongue.[5] Your words bring gifts like comfort and laughter to our lives. As a Six, you have a unique way with words. Riso and Hudson point out, "Sixes know how to arouse strong emotional responses in others, engaging their emotions unconsciously. They have the capacity to get people to respond to them."[6]

I have found this to be true with my healthy Six friends. They are often prophetic, agitating for change by stirring up my emotions and sparking my conscience about the things God cares about. When you share your convictions, it gets my adrenaline going! On a lighter note, my wife Lindsey, the funniest person I know, and my ten-year-old son Zane, move me to laughter daily with their wit—a sign Sixes feel secure with others and desire intimacy. Healthy Loyalists seem to have the gift of turning anxiety into humor at the drop of a dime, making our lives more playful (and mischievous).[7]

You've been given the ministry of words. What you say, good and bad, sticks around. The wrong ones can be forgiven, yes, but they aren't always easily forgotten. Conversely, the right words don't just have the power to describe someone's reality, but change it forever.

---

### → Pray

Father, help me put away "anger, wrath, malice, slander, and obscene talk from [my] mouth."[8] I'm thankful that "The grass withers, the flower fades, but the word of our God will stand forever."[9] Your Word continually brings hope, assurance, and peace to my life. Give me life-giving words to say today to build up others in a way they'll never forget.

---

5   Proverbs 18:21

6   Riso and Hudson, *Personality Types*, 228.

7   Ibid., 229.

8   Colossians 3:8

9   Isaiah 40:8

# Day 34 Reflections:

**What is the greatest compliment or piece of encouragement you've ever received?**

**Who have you caught yourself blaming for the problems in your life? What might you need to confess or seek forgiveness for?**

**How can you grow in being an encouragement to others?**

---

**→ Respond**

Meditate on a recent outburst of anger. Are you angry because someone left their dishes on the table, you had a bad day at work, you feel overwhelmed, or you are taking on too much? Spend time processing your own feelings before starting an argument.

# The Discipline of Remembering

*Bless the Lord, O my soul, and forget not all his benefits, who forgives all your*

*iniquity, who heals all your diseases, who redeems your life from the pit, who*

*crowns you with steadfast love and mercy, who satisfies you with good so that*

*your youth is renewed like the eagle's.*

—Proverbs 103:2-5

IMAGINE WALKING INTO YOUR FAVORITE LOCAL SANDWICH shop and coming to the realization that it's a one-woman operation. She's the owner, cashier, sandwich maker, and janitor all in one. Though she's always making sandwiches for her growing number of customers, she never seems to eat. As months of lunch breaks go by, you notice she's beginning to look unhealthy. Once energetic, she now looks pale and exhausted. Though the shop has an abundance of food, she is forgetting to feed herself.[2]

> The opposite of home is not distance, but forgetfulness.
>
> –Elie Wiesel[1]

---

1   Chestnut, *The Complete Enneagram*, 57.

2   Illustration adapted from Tim Ellmore, "The Starving Baker for Teachers," Growing Leaders, September 9, 2011, https://growingleaders.com/blog/the-starving-baker-for-teachers/.

Like the starving baker in this illustration, unhealthy Loyalists may become physically, emotionally, and spiritually malnourished when they forget to take care of themselves. Do you feel guilty for putting others on hold to practice self-care? Don't shortchange yourself by thinking your needs or self-development are not worth the trouble; you are God's beloved and He cares about how you are doing before He cares about who you are helping.

Sixes' attention is continually pulled outward, keeping them from exploring the contours of their own soul. But healthy Sixes make it a priority to remember their own needs and desires, becoming a healthier version of themselves for their families and organizations. Don't wait until you experience a mental breakdown to pursue self-care, but be proactive with your health like this Six has: "I have been focusing my attention on growing flowers as opposed to pulling weeds all the time."[3] Rather than waiting for the weeds to pop up, what are you planting today to help yourself grow and flourish?

> Sixes tend to suffer from amnesia about their past wins, successes, and accomplishments.

Doing something physical is a good way to straighten out circular thinking and build determination—for example, caring for the flowers you have planted. Give your mind some much-needed relief from over-analyzing what might happen and instead go make something positive happen by allocating more time in your life for a hobby, entertainment, or exercise. Cultivating your creative side is another strategic way to diffuse your mental energy. Former President George W. Bush, who has been said to be a Loyalist, took up the hobby of painting after his time in office and now does it every single day as a form of self-care.

The most important remembering you must do above all is meditating on God's past and present care for you. Sixes tend to suffer from amnesia about their past wins, successes, and accomplishments—which leads to low self-esteem or a lack of confidence in the present. That's why the Bible is littered with stories of people being commanded to remember.

---

3   Riso and Hudson, *The Wisdom*, 257.

Moses commanded the people of Israel, "Only take care, and keep your soul diligently, lest you forget the things that your eyes have seen, and lest they depart from your heart all the days of your life. Make them known to your children and your children's children."[4]

After miraculously crossing the Jordan, Joshua sets up an altar and says, "When your children ask in time to come, 'What do these stones mean to you?' then you shall tell them that the waters of the Jordan were cut off before the ark of the covenant of the LORD. ... So these stones shall be to the people of Israel a memorial forever."[5]

Before leaving them to follow his call to the cross, Jesus charges His followers to remember His presence and self-giving love through the sharing of the bread and the cup: "And he took bread, gave thanks and broke it, and gave it to them, saying, 'This is my body given for you; do this in remembrance of me.' "[6]

Likewise, how will you lay your stones of remembrance? How will you create more space in your life to actively remember God's provision and presence? Remember, the key to building more self-confidence and living with a peaceful mind starts with cultivating an attitude of gratitude.

***The Good News for Loyalists*** is that there is always something to be grateful for. The psalmist exhorts us to "forget not" our God who forgives, heals, redeems, crowns, satisfies, and renews. You are magnificent to Him, and He has done great things for you and through you—all you have to do today is remember. Spend time writing in your journal today about how God has been faithful to you. Begin your personal conversations and team meetings today with the question: "Where have we seen God's faithfulness?"

---

4   Deuteronomy 4:9

5   Joshua 4:6-7

6   Luke 22:19 NIV

> ### → Pray
>
> Father, You have forgiven my sins and redeemed my life from the pit. With the Spirit's help, I will remember all You've done for me and model a celebratory life. Because You care for me, I will make it a priority to care for myself so others can have the best version of me. Help me to rejoice always and give thanks in all circumstances.[7]

# Day 35 Reflections:

**What do you need most right now to be healthy?**

_______________________________________________

_______________________________________________

_______________________________________________

_______________________________________________

**How does your schedule need to change for you to prioritize self-care?**

_______________________________________________

_______________________________________________

_______________________________________________

_______________________________________________

**What has God done in your life that you will share with future generations? Name your stones of remembrance.**

_______________________________________________

_______________________________________________

_______________________________________________

_______________________________________________

> ### → Respond
>
> Keep a record in your journal of all your God-wins and personal successes. Keep coming back to this list as a way to boost your self-confidence and future hope.

---

7   1 Thessalonians 5:16-18

*Day 36:*

# The Wolf Pack

*My sheep hear my voice, and I know them, and they follow me. I give them*

*eternal life, and they will never perish, and no one will snatch them out*

*of my hand.*

—John 10:27-28

WOLVES TEND TO ORGANIZE THEMSELVES INTO PACKS, living and hunting together in organized groups across a broad range of countryside rather than trying to survive separately. The term *wolf pack* has come to symbolize a group of people that is bonded together by loyalty and true devotion; few people express this instinct for communal survival like this type. Loyalists often view their church not as a business or an organization as others might, but as a wolf pack that has each other's backs. They give themselves, body and soul, for the pack—as long as the pack continues to protect them.

> For the strength of the Pack is the Wolf, and the strength of the Wolf is the Pack.
>
> —Rudyard Kipling[1]

In our individualistic "me first" society, it's the Sixes who swim upstream to fight for the

---

1  Scott Peterson and Joshua Pruett, *The Jungle Book: The Strength of the Wolf is the Pack* (United States: Disney Book Group, 2016).

preservation of our churches and social institutions, sticking around even when perfection is far out of reach. As Cron and Stabile beautifully share, "[Sixes] won't leave a church if they're not 'being fed,' the announcements are too long, the church has gotten too big (or too small), the music is (fill in the blank), or they don't agree with everything the pastor says from the pulpit. Sixes are the most loyal number on the Enneagram."[2]

Sixes are necessary for any institution or community. They are the German Shepherds of the Enneagram: teachable, attentive, and fiercely loyal. However, this also means Sixes need to be on guard for any unhealthy tendencies in their relationship with authority. It's been said that every wolf pack has an "alpha wolf" that fights their way to the top. Similarly, churches also have alpha leaders—but not every leader is trustworthy. As Jesus said, "Beware of false prophets, who come to you in sheep's clothing but inwardly are ravenous wolves."[3] These selfish wolves control others through fear and demand unquestioning loyalty. And, as we've said previously, Sixes make classic prophets—strong, clear-headed, and loving enough to raise a warning flag. They are often the first to call out these false shepherds when their true colors appear.

> Giving your ultimate allegiance to Jesus may mean you have to question your leader at times or your group's belief-system.

However, while Loyalists desire justice, they also come with an exaggerated need for security, which means the average Six may find themselves drawn to authoritarian leaders, or forms of community with hard and fast rules and airtight doctrines. (In some cases, we find fundamentalist churches to be full of unhealthy Loyalists being led along by a charismatic authoritarian.) An unhealthy Six may willingly put themselves in a subordinate position and turn "over all of their inner guidance, judgment, and power to this authority."[4] When this happens, the Six will resort to doing their duty like a good soldier without asking any questions. I heard one Counterphobic Six lament how he became

---

2  Cron and Stabile, *The Road Back to You*, 193.

3  Matthew 7:15

4  Maitri, *The Spiritual Dimension*, 80-81.

the executive assistant of a well-known megachurch pastor to conquer his fear and "get close to Caesar" but was eventually chewed up and spat out by his compassionless boss.

Sometimes true loyalty means breaking free from codependency or blind obedience to an unhealthy person or group. Giving your ultimate allegiance to Jesus may mean you have to question your leader at times or your group's belief-system. Have you drawn your own conclusions from study, prayer, and experience, or do you simply follow the current authority in your life? A healthy Six won't be afraid to explore the world beyond their "tribe," and one of the best things you can do is study other ways of thinking and participate in groups outside your comfort zone to cultivate discernment. Like a flu shot, injecting yourself with something that may feel "harmful" from the outside may actually strengthen your faith in the long run.

***The Good News for Loyalists*** is that Jesus is your Chief Shepherd. Jesus offers you His loving protection through the local church; it's the place for His sheep to be known, fed, led, and cared for. He places "undershepherds"—leaders called to lay down their lives for the sheep and set a godly example—in authority over local churches. Though we know there are unhealthy outliers, there are many leaders you can trust. Once you've found your "pack," seek to be a leader, not just a follower. One of your greatest gifts to the body of Christ is launching and leading safe and nurturing environments that help people thrive. Don't just dream about the kind of church you want to be part of, go make it happen!

---

### → Pray

Father, thank You for being my Chief Shepherd who drives away the false prophets with Your staff. Give me the discernment to spot these wolves whenever they appear. You have my full trust and loyalty, and I will not bend my knee to any other earthly leader. Use me to help build a safe and healthy church community right where I am.

# Day 36 Reflections:

**How have you caught yourself either overestimating an authority figure or placing your trust in someone who turns out to be untrustworthy?**

**What might pledging your ultimate allegiance to Jesus mean for your relationships or community involvement?**

**When have you experienced God's loving protection through the church? Are there any negative experiences that you still need healing from? Explain.**

---

**→ Respond**

Even if you don't see yourself as a self-starter, take the initiative in your ministry or workplace to start a Bible study, discipleship group, support group, or counseling ministry.

*Day 37:*

# Lie Detector

*For he knows the secrets of the heart.*

—Psalm 44:21b

BELIEVE IT OR NOT, MOST PEOPLE LIE every day. A 2002 study published in the *Journal of Basic and Applied Social Psychology* said 60% of the participants were found to lie at least one time during a 10-minute conversation. University of Massachusetts psychologist Robert Feldman, who conducted the study, said, "It was a very surprising result. We didn't expect lying to be such a common part of daily life."[2] Perhaps you agree with Feldman's surprise, but if you're a Six, you're most likely shaking your head right now thinking, "Actually, I do expect people to lie everyday!"

> But better to get hurt by the truth than be comforted with a lie.
>
> –Khaled Hosseini[1]

Loyalists have a built-in lie detector. Beatrice Chestnut describes the Six as having the superpower of "seeing through false pretenses and detecting ulterior motives

---

1   Khaled Hosseini, *The Kite Runner: Rejacketed* (India: Bloomsbury, 2011), 50.

2   "UMass Researcher Finds Most People Lie in Everyday Conversation," ScienceDaily (ScienceDaily, June 12, 2002), http://www.sciencedaily.com/releases/2002/06/020611070813.htm.

and hidden agendas."[3] They don't trust appearances, but ask many questions, constantly testing others' words for authenticity and genuineness. My friend Becky (a Six) told me that, as she is listening to someone, she finds herself silently asking: "What are you saying? Why are you saying it? Do I trust you?"

Sixes carry their own mental polygraph machine with them wherever they go because they simply want the truth, the whole truth, and nothing but the truth. Safety—their greatest desire—lies in full disclosure. Even bad news is a gift for them compared to doctored or withheld information, and secrecy or manipulation is their "unpardonable sin." When Lindsey and I purchased our current home, the seller's disclosure stated that nothing was structurally wrong with the house, but a year later, after continued leaks in our basement, I called a local company to get an estimate. This happened to be the same company that had come to our house four months before we purchased it and offered the previous owners an estimate for the problem. This older estimate revealed an image of mold, which had now spread throughout the entire basement. The long, aggravating, and expensive legal journey that followed to eventually fix the issue exhausted us physically and emotionally.

> Jesus came to bring justice to the cunning deceivers of the world.

Thankfully, Jesus came to bring justice to the cunning deceivers of the world. No one cares more about the truth than God—and, unlike the 80-to-90 percent effectiveness of even the best lie detector, His lie detector is fool-proof. As the psalmist rhetorically asks, "Would not God discover this? For he knows the secrets of the heart."[4] Ultimately, it's not all up to us to catch every fake and inauthenticity we encounter, and our zeal for truth can sometimes even backfire. C.S. Lewis warns skeptics, "You cannot go on 'seeing through' things forever. The whole point of seeing through something is to see something through it."[5]

There was once a man named Nathanael who had spent his life "seeing through people." When his friend, Phillip, shows up and tells Nathanael that the Messiah has come after all these years, you can hear the skepticism in his reply: "Nazareth!

---

3   Chestnut, *The Complete Enneagram*, 185.

4   Psalm 44:21

5   C.S. Lewis, *The Abolition of Man* (New York: Macmillan, 1947, 1965), 91.

Can anything good come from there?"[6] Nathanael's snobbery (and probably a lifetime of correctly identifying falsehoods) gets in the way of him receiving the real truth—at first.

***The Good News for Loyalists*** is that our trustworthy Father sent His Son to protect us from the "father of lies"[7] so that the truth may set us free. Furthermore, Jesus is patient with our skepticism. When Jesus sees Nathanael approaching, He says of him, "Behold, an Israelite indeed, in whom there is no deceit!" Puzzled, Nathanael asked, "How do you know me?" Jesus responds, "Before Philip called you, when you were under the fig tree, I saw you." Then Nathanel declares, "Rabbi, you are the Son of God! You are the King of Israel!"[8] In a beautiful turn of events, this suspicious skeptic-turned-believer now abandons himself fully to "the way, the truth, and the life."[9]

---

### → Pray

Father, thank You for giving me the gift of seeing through deception. But I confess, there are times I've been wrong. Help me not to miss the truth when it is standing in front of me. If Satan can't get me through his lies, he'll come after me with cynicism. So, help me to use my discernment to lead myself and others out of endless questioning and toward the truth.

---

6   John 1:46 NIV

7   John 8:44

8   John 1:46-49

9   John 14:6 NIV

# Day 37 Reflections:

**How has your lie detector saved you in the past?**

**When has your skepticism led you to feel lonely, anxious, distant from God, or standing on the wrong side?**

**How will you use your gift of discernment to lead others to the truth rather than get stuck in cynicism?**

---

**→ Respond**

Audit your relationship. Skeptics tend to go to other skeptics. You might feel better after engaging in a complaining session, but it won't take you any farther. Consider the impact of your social relationships.

# Trusting God with Your Family

*[God] said, "Take your son, your only son Isaac, whom you love, and go to the land of Moriah, and offer him there as a burnt offering on one of the mountains of which I shall tell you."*

—Genesis 22:2

THERE AREN'T MANY PASSAGES IN THE BIBLE that make Lindsey cringe as much as this one. What would you say if God asked you to give up one of your closest family members? Well, in one of Scripture's foundational narratives, God asks Abraham to do just that—to take his only son, the son of promise, and offer him as a sacrifice. Though this story sounds barbaric to our modern ears, it would've been par for the course in this ancient Near Eastern context—just another story of the gods asking for everything from their worshipers.

> Let your children go if you want to keep them.
>
> –Malcom Forbes[1]

Loyalists, as you can infer from the title, make for the most fiercely committed family members. Family is not an afterthought, but a first thought. Sixes make incredible parents, caregivers,

---

1  Malcom Forbes, *The Sayings of Chairman Malcom: The Capitalist's Handbook* (United States: Harper & Row, 1978).

mentors, and considerate leaders. Author Jacqui Pollock teaches that Sixes give their loved ones a sense of safety with their penchant for preparedness. They radiate warmth, compassion, and genuine care along with a good dose of humor and wit. They model what it looks like to fight for the underdog and protect the vulnerable. Their reliability and highly detail-oriented nature tends to bring positive results on their tasks and projects.[2]

On the other hand, as with anything in our lives, family can become an idol—a good thing that turns into a god-thing. Timothy Keller teaches that an idol is anything that absorbs your heart and mind more than God, becoming "so central and essential to your life that, should you lose it, your life would feel hardly worth living."[3]

> Faith puts our need for safety on the altar because safety is not always God's highest priority.

When someone becomes an idol in our lives, we end up placing "god-like" expectations on them too heavy for anyone to bear. Pollock explains that a Six's constant worrying about their loved one's safety can become smothering, often leading to rebellion in later years. Additionally, when Sixes begin to project their fears onto their loved ones, it may lead to a lack of confidence or ability to cope with life—for both the Six and the person on whom they're projecting. Finally, when Sixes feel unsure or insecure on the inside, they may become authoritarian or confrontational—their gift of dutifulness can spiral into a constant demand to follow the rules, which feels restrictive and stifling to everyone around them.[4]

On the bright side, when Sixes are healthy, they will loosen their grip on others. They will step back, have more fun, and allow their loved ones to fight their own battles. They will hold rules more loosely, take risks, be flexible, and help others learn it's okay to make mistakes, displaying to everyone that obeying the spirit of the law is more important than its letter. They will find ways to manage their stress and relieve anxiety—a Counterphobic Six will even drop their

---

2  Pollock, *Knowing Me, Knowing Them*, 114.

3  Timothy Keller, *Counterfeit Gods: The Empty Promises of Money, Sex, and Power, and the Only Hope That Matters* (United States: Penguin Publishing Group, 2011), XX.

4  Pollock, *Knowing Me, Knowing Them*, 116-117.

intimidating mask and begin to share their fears—which lowers the stress level for everyone around.[5]

***The Good News for Loyalists*** is God knows what's best for your family. Will you be brave enough to trust and release them into the arms of their loving Creator? Their entire well-being is dependent on whether or not you release your plans for them into God's hands. Years ago, I led overseas mission trips with college students, and, inevitably, some parents wouldn't allow their young but adult children to come with us. They just couldn't let them go into the world's uncertainty. It's true you must protect your loved ones from danger, but when God calls us to obey, we are called to trust as Abraham—no matter how illogical it feels from a human standpoint. Faith puts our need for safety on the altar because safety is not always God's highest priority.

Abraham, with trembling hands, takes the knife and stretches out his hands to sacrifice his son Isaac. At the last minute, the Lord stops him, saying, "Do not lay your hand on the boy or do anything to him, for now I know that you fear God, seeing you have not withheld your son, your only son, from me."[6] Does this sound familiar? Today, we can say we know God loves us because He did not withhold His only Son, the Son of Promise. You can trust God with your loved one because God already gave you His.

---

### → Pray

Father, thank You for giving me such a strong commitment to my family. Help me remember that You know what's best for them. Loosen my grip so I won't get in the way of them being used mightily for Your purposes. I will surrender all of my fears to you today regarding my family.

---

5   Ibid., 121-124.

6   Genesis 22:12

# Day 38 Reflections:

**How have your strengths of care and commitment positively influenced your family?**

**In what ways have you seen over-protectiveness, insecurities, or authoritarianism negatively affect your family?**

**Which family member do you need to let go of in order to fully entrust them to the Lord?**

> ### → Respond
>
> Create an "I Surrender" list, and name all the fears or anxieties you can think of regarding one family member: a wandering faith, uncertain future, unhealthy habits, devastating diagnosis, toxic friendships, and so on. Then surrender all those things to God in prayer.

# Hope for the Hopeless

*May the God of hope fill you with all joy and peace in believing, so that by the*

*power of the Holy Spirit you may abound in hope.*

—Romans 15:13

GOD'S PLANS ARE MOST OFTEN ACCOMPLISHED IN the quiet dark without our knowing. One of the most bizarre stories in the Old Testament is found in 1 Samuel. The ark of the covenant has been stolen by Israel's enemies, the Philistines. (This was, of course, many years before Indiana Jones saved it from the Nazis!) This priceless, gold-plated chest held the two tablets of the law given to Moses by God, among other things, and sat in the tabernacle within the Holy of Holies, where God's divine presence dwelled in the midst of the people.

> There are no hopeless situations; there are only people who have grown hopeless about them.
>
> —Clare Boothe Luce

One day, after Israel lost four thousand soldiers to the Philistines, they brought out the ark of the covenant to the battlefield, desperately hoping the presence of God would bring victory. Long story short, the Philistines kill thirty thousand more Israelite soldiers and steal the priceless ark. The Israelites can't begin to comprehend how they will move on after this devastating blow. They are without hope and feel as if God's presence has—literally—departed.[1]

But the story doesn't end there. The Philistines put the ark in their temple next to a statue of their god, Dagon, and in the morning, are surprised to find it toppled over. After setting their god upright, the very next morning they discover Dagon again toppled. Naturally fearful, they decide to offload this bad luck charm to their neighbors in Gath, but once there, things take a turn for the worst when the citizens start getting tumors[2] (some believe the Hebrew translates to hemorrhoids).[3]

Having had enough, Gath offloads the ark onto their neighbors in Ekron. But once in Ekron, their people start dying of plague. At this point, the humbled Philistines give in and overnight it back to the Israelites. After the ark comes rolling back into the city, on an unmanned cart, the city erupts with praise. I'm sure every Israelite remembered exactly where they were that day when they heard the news that "God's presence" had returned.[4]

> God is always fighting our battles—right before our eyes and behind enemy lines.

Life changing, hope-filled news tends to stick around. I still remember celebrating Lindsey's birthday in that Village Inn when we got the call from the Child Savings Institute about a newborn baby in the NICU with no one to take him home. Soon after, we were able to meet our son Zane for the very first time on what happened to be Lindsey's and my date-iversary.

For years, we felt hopeless like the Israelites. Our precious dream of raising a family felt stolen or at least perpetually delayed. God's life-giving presence had left us, and we waited, waited, and waited some more. We didn't know it at the time, but God was working in our waiting. Just as God was working in this story—in the dark, behind enemy lines, and unbeknownst to a single Israelite—

---

1   1 Samuel 4:1-22

2   1 Samuel 5

3   "H6076 - ʿōp̄el - Strong's Hebrew Lexicon (KJV)," Blue Letter Bible, accessed October 23, 2021, https://www.blueletterbible.org/lexicon/h6076/kjv/wlc/0-1/.

4   1 Samuel 5:8–6:21

so too was God working for us, forming a new, beautiful life in the womb for nine whole months while we sat and wondered if God was listening to us.

When all seems hopeless, it's reassuring to know God is always fighting our battles—right before our eyes and behind enemy lines. God may have already answered your prayer and a call is on the way. But even if it's not, you can rejoice knowing God's presence as conveyed through His people is the true answer to prayer.

***The Good News for Loyalists*** is there are no hopeless situations for God's children. On the cross, Jesus turned the greatest tragedy into a triumph and He will do the same for you when your life doesn't go as planned. The God of hope is ever-present in your life, giving you a peace that transcends your deepest fears and what-ifs. By the power of the Holy Spirit dwelling within you and binding this world together, He will conquer any cynicism within that begs you to give up on prayer to protect your heart. If you feel desperate or downcast today, open your heart wide and let God fill you with hope.

---

### → Pray

Father, thank You for filling me with hope when I don't have any. Just as Jesus, after His resurrection, walked alongside the downcast disciples on the road to Emmaus and filled them with hope, draw near and remind me that all will be well. By faith, I choose to believe You are working even if I can't see how. I will trust Your promises and wait on you.

# Day 39 Reflections:

**Where do you feel hopeless? Where do you feel hopeful?**

**When has God protected you by not giving you what you asked for?**

**How does Jesus's resurrection speak to your hopeless situations?**

> **→ Respond**
>
> Contact someone you know who is in a hopeless situation right now and seek to strengthen them through your caring presence.

*Day 40:*

# Walking on Water

*And Peter answered him, "Lord, if it is you, command me to come to you on the*

*water." He said, "Come." So Peter got out of the boat and walked on the water*

*and came to Jesus.*

—Matthew 14:28-29

As we wrap up this incredible 40-day journey, I want to end by reflecting once more on the life of the apostle Peter, who I think of as the patron saint of all Sixes. Peter's new life begins on the shores of the sea when Jesus says, "Follow me, and I will make you fishers of men."[2] As a Loyalist, you know how hard it would be to drop that net.

> If you want to walk on water, you've got to get out of the boat.
>
> –John Ortberg[1]

The "safety nets" we carry around with our old identity, addictions, relationships, or defensive strategies appear to provide insurance and assurance. But, they must be let go to follow Jesus for "It is better to take

---

1  John Ortberg, *If You Want to Walk on Water, You've Got to Get Out of the Boat* (United States: Zondervan, 2001).

2  Matthew 4:19

refuge in the LORD than to trust in man."[3] Ask yourself, "What net am I still carrying around? Am I more concerned with establishing and maintaining my safety, than pursuing God's aspirations?" Can you imagine how different Peter's life would have been if he had played it safe?

By God's grace, Jesus turned Peter's cowardice into courage and his toughness into vulnerability, but it took some time. Once, when Peter and the disciples were in a boat in the middle of a storm, they looked out and saw Jesus walking on the sea. Acting in true counterphobic fashion, Peter decides to be the first to confront his fear head-on saying, "Lord, if it is you, command me to come to you on the water."[4] Please take note that the type Six disciple is the first to get out of the boat!

But as soon as Peter steps out onto the sea and sees the gusting wind, he becomes terribly and (understandably) afraid and cries out, "Lord, save me." So Jesus reaches out, rescuing Peter and following up with a rebuke: "Why did you doubt?"[5] The obvious answer to that question is that Peter took his eyes off of Jesus and got distracted by his circumstances. But equally important, Peter, the Loyalist, doubted Jesus had given him the power to walk on water without His or the other disciples' help. Whether you are feeling phobic (and want to hide under an oar) or counterphobic (I'll jump now and freak out later), Jesus wants to instill in you all the confidence you need to walk across the sea of all that feels downright impossible. You can do it.

> What would you do if you had nothing to fear?

***The Good News for Loyalists*** is "if we are faithless, he remains faithful—for he cannot deny himself."[6] I know you can be hard on yourself for all the "shoulda, woulda, couldas" in your life, but don't be! No matter how many times Jesus has had to take you by the hand when you were sinking, He is faithful even when you

---

3   Psalm 118:8

4   Matthew 14:24-28

5   Matthew 14:29-31

6   2 Timothy 2:13

are faithless and will never give up on you because you belong to Him. When Jesus returns for us in the end, we will call Him "Faithful and True."[7]

Let me ask perhaps the most important question in this whole book: What would you do if you had nothing to fear? Write a book, do public speaking, foster or adopt, switch careers, leave the country, go to law school, serve your country, or take a stand for others? What would you do if you had the same level of confidence that God has in you right now? Just as the disciples needed Peter's courage then to lead the first century church through trial and persecution, we need your courage now more than ever. Don't worry. You don't need to have everything figured out. Today, you just need to get out of the boat.

### ➜ Pray

Father, I am certain that death nor life, nor anything else in all creation will be able to separate me from Your love.[8] When I walk through the dark valley, I will not bow down to fear, for You are right there with me.[9] Help me to live my life with purpose and great strength. Because "your steadfast love is better than life, my lips will praise you."[10]

---

7   Revelation 19:11

8   Romans 8:38-39

9   Psalm 23:4

10   Psalm 63:3

# Day 40 Reflections:

**What safety net do you need to leave behind to run after Jesus?**

**What would you do if you had nothing to fear?**

**How do you want the world to remember you?**

---

### → Respond

Find a life coach or spiritual mentor to come alongside and support you in accomplishing your goals. Start working courageously toward something today that seems impossible without God's supernatural power and grace.

FATHER, I AM DEEPLY GRATEFUL TO YOU for creating me in Your image as Your beloved child. You created me to specifically reflect Your courage and faithfulness. I confess I've lived too often for my own security, putting too much faith in my plans, belief systems, or authorities. I have found myself at times being paranoid, hypervigilant, reactive, self-doubtful, and either too submissive or too rebellious. You, being rich in mercy, saw me from heaven and sent Your faithful Son, Jesus, to die on the cross for my faithlessness. Now, I revel in the fact that You will never abandon me and have given me eternal security. Clothed with the power of the Holy Spirit, I will view safety not as an end, but the means to a better end— pursuing all of Your bold aspirations for my life. Putting off cowardice and self-protection and putting on my new self that is made in Christ's image, I will not shy away from success, but will steward the courage You've given me to shower the world with Christ's fierce loyalty and protection.

# Three Types of Loyalists

BELOW IS A SUMMARY OF THE THREE types of Sixes (called subtypes) from the teaching of Beatrice Chestnut, whose book, *The Complete Enneagram* covers all twenty-seven subtypes of the main nine Enneagram types.[1] As discussed in the introduction, these subtypes are helpful in drilling down the different nuances of the Loyalist, which can vary so wildly that at times you may wonder how someone with those traits could even be the same type as you!

Warning: many of these descriptions will seem overly negative. However, one of the main purposes of the Enneagram is to help us discover our "shadow self"— the ways we interact with the world unconsciously and often in times of stress. These descriptions are not indictments; rather, they are a further opportunity to deepen our awareness of how to interact with the world.

## The Self-Preservation Six

The Self-Preservation Six is the most fearful, a trait that often manifests as insecurity. This subtype experiences a lot of indecisiveness, uncertainty, and hesitation. They doubt themselves more than anyone else and ask many unanswerable questions. They fear disappointing others and flee from anger, aggression, and confrontation, and they have a driving need to secure protection through alliances and friendships by being friendly, trustworthy, and supportive. They distrust themselves as capable in this dangerous world and therefore seek refuge in a strong person or group for support and guidance. This Six tends to experience separation anxiety and will use their warmth and friendliness to prevent being abandoned. Like Ones, they believe that being good means repressing anger. On the outside, they appear warm and peaceful, but under the surface they feel fear, guilt, and anguish. They are "heart-centered" on the outside but "head-centered" on the inside. Because they are so friendly and build relationships well, these Sixes can look like Type Twos—the only difference being that Sixes want safety, whereas Twos want approval.

---

1   Beatrice Chestnut, *The Complete Enneagram: 27 Paths to Greater Self-Knowledge* (Berkeley, CA: She Writes Press, 2013).

## The Social Six

Where the Self-Preservation Six appears soft, warm, friendly, informal, and uncertain, the Social Six appears stronger, cooler, formal, shy, and certain. They have a mixture of phobic and counterphobic expressions (see a list of tendencies on page eight) and cope with their anxiety by relying on their authority of reason, guidelines, rules, rational thinking, high ideals, or institutions. The Social Six has a more black and white view of life and can be almost "too sure" or fanatical about their beliefs or convictions at times. Intolerant of ambiguity, they constantly need clear categories so they can know who the good and bad guys are; they love diagrams and flowcharts. The Social Six anticipates the worst more than the other two subtypes, and therefore painstakingly strives to know the rules of the game. They are the most responsible of the three subtypes, are rule-followers who do their duty for the common good, and fear disapproval from the "good" authorities. A Social Six may look like a Type One in that they may be controlling, impatient, and critical, wanting people to do things their way. However, Ones are guided by their own internal standards while Social Sixes adhere to external codes.

## The One-To-One Six

The One-To-One Six is the most Counterphobic Six. More than the other subtypes, they believe the world to be dangerous and will do everything possible not to feel cheated, attacked, or taken advantage of. They are "the countertype" (which means they don't look like the typical Six) and might get confused with Type Eights. Like Eights, these Sixes appear "hot," strong, and intimidating (although they might be unaware of their intensity), and believe the best defense is a good offense. However, Eights are fearless while Sixes are motivated by fear. Additionally, another difference is that Eights like order, but One-To-One Sixes tend to disrupt order. They give off the appearance of being a tough rebel or troublemaker to keep their enemies from attacking. They move toward their fears to conquer them—feeling safer when they put themselves in dangerous situations rather than hiding from them. They are the most scared standing still, so they convince themselves that they can erase their fears if they are confronted. Rather than thinking in best-case or worst-case terms, they tend to be the contrarian who always argues the opposite side as everyone else. This Six is the least aware of their fear and must pay attention to the ways it manifests as anger, aggression, or assertiveness.

# Next Steps

I'M SO PROUD OF YOU FOR FINISHING this 40-day journey. That's a big accomplishment! Though this book isn't small by any means, you may feel (like me) that we've only begun to explore the tip of the iceberg. You're probably wondering: *What now? My eyes have been opened, I've grown in greater self-awareness and empathy, and now I'm ready to take the next step!* Here are some ideas::

1. Follow "Gospel for Enneagram" on Instagram, Facebook, or Twitter to continue learning and engaging.

2. Download my free resource called *Should Christians Use The Enneagram?* at gospelforenneagram.com.

3. If you found this book helpful, please leave an honest review (or star rating) online or share on social media so others can find it.

4. Visit my website, gospelforenneagram.com, to find more helpful links and resources.

5. Join a church community where you can continue to grow in your knowledge of God and self. To go the distance, find a mentor, coach, or support system.

6. Ask a friend, spouse, or mentor to meet regularly with you to discuss the insights God has revealed to you through this book. Invite them, along with your small group, to get a devotional on their Enneagram type and share what they learn with you.

7. Email me with any thoughts, questions, or feedback to tyler@gospelforenneagram.com. I'd love to hear from you!

# Acknowledgements

My wife: Lindsey, you show me the gospel every day by loving me for who I am and not what I do. Thank you for your tremendous encouragement to be a writer and for bearing with my workaholic tendencies. I want to be more like you.

My editors: Joshua, thank you for bringing your incredible creativity to the table. Your re-rewrites helped elevate my writing to a whole new level. Stephanie, your attention to detail and passion for this project gave me tremendous confidence. Lee Ann, your veteran experience and thoroughness increased the value of this book tremendously.

My coach: John Fooshee, thank you for your Enneagram coaching and partnership. I'm deeply grateful for your willingness to come alongside me and put wind in my sails.

My influences: I wouldn't have been able to pull this off without a multitude of direct and indirect influences such as pastors, teachers, and writers (including you, mom!) over the years. I'm deeply grateful for the spiritual heroes that have come before me and shaped me.

# www.GospelForEnneagram.com